Cover and Title

Revealing

God wants all Christians to **reveal** the truth found in Scriptures about all issues, including those associated with homosexuality and gender change. If we are ostracized or greatly criticized for what we do or say in this regard, then we must be willing to bear the consequences, for everyone deserves to hear the truth about these issues.

Pray on my behalf, that utterance may be given to me in the opening of my mouth, to make known with boldness the mystery of the gospel, for which I am an ambassador in chains; that in proclaiming it I may speak boldly, as I ought to speak. Ephesians 6:19-20

God's Design

A prominent view in western culture today is to discredit **God's design** for mankind. But according to Scripture, God is perfect in what He designs, from the beauty of a **butterfly** to the creating of a man and a woman. Without this design in play, society will continue to drift in a sea of meaningless relativity where everyone does whatever is right in their own eyes. Males attracted to males, females drawn to females, males becoming females, or females changing into males, or some version of the above.

God designed each of us with amazingly complex DNA mapping, chromosomes, and genetic material to produce a unique person with all the personality characteristics that blueprint a wonderful child of God. Medically altering the body does not change this unique DNA. God has given us good scientists who help repair the disfigurements that sin has placed on this world and our own bodies. Do we have the right to reject God's sexual identity and design for our life? It is we who make a mistake and bring confusion, conflict, and misunderstanding to our world when we try to change or alter what He has designed.

> *God created man in His own image, in the image of God He created him; both male and female He created them. Genesis 1:27*

With Love

As we reveal to others the truth about God's design for a man and a woman, we must do it with a great deal of **love** and grace, the same kind Jesus modeled for all of us while on earth. Without this love then all that we say or do about homosexuality and gender change becomes like a noisy gong or a clanging cymbal to others, rather than a comforting message of hope and salvation.

> *If I speak with the tongues of men and of angels but do not have love, I have become a noisy gong or a clanging cymbal. Love bears all things, believes all things, hopes all things, endures all things. I Corinthians 13: 1, 7*

With Gratitude

Again I say to you, that if two of you agree on earth about anything that they may ask, it shall be done for them by My Father who is in heaven. For where two or three have gathered together in My name, I am there in their midst. Matthew 18:20-21

A great deal of thanks goes to all who took my manuscript and fine-tuned it with their excellent editing skills, Biblical insights, and wise suggestions. In their different ways, each made this book better than what it would have been without their contribution.

These special friends and family members include Myrna, Linus, Don, Keith, Ralph, Catherine, Rick, Brodie, Paul, Gilbert, and Jim.

Copyright 2019 Kent McClain
Web site -www.tmoments.com
Published by *Destinee Media (*March 2019)
Cover design: Myrna Winnian Sleath

Other books by Kent McClain

Teachable Moments
(Teaching Children How to Remember God's Truth)

Sowing Teachable Moments
(Memorable and Interactive Lessons to help Children Remember God's Truth)

What Was I Thinking?
(Learning an Ocean of Grace in a Pond of Legalism)

Mission Possible
(The Sequence of How Jesus Discipled the 12)
Currently out of print

Table of Contents

Homosexuality, Transgender People, and the Scriptures	Chapter 1
Born Homosexual	Chapter 2
"Coming out"	Chapter 3
Homophobia	Chapter 4
Worse Than Other Sins	Chapter 5
Jesus and Gays	Chapter 6
God's Judgment and Sexual Disease	Chapter 7
Christians Who Adopt the Gay Lifestyle or Change Gender	Chapter 8
Judging the LGBT Community	Chapter 9
Churches that Validate the LGBT Agenda	Chapter 10
Government Leaders, Justices, and Educators that Legislate for the LGBT agenda	Chapter 11
Hollywood and the Media's Push	Chapter 12
Reaching Out and Loving the LGBT Community	Chapter 13
Conclusion (Last questions)	Chapter 14
Questions from the Chapters	Appendix

With Gratitude

Again I say to you, that if two of you agree on earth about anything that they may ask, it shall be done for them by My Father who is in heaven. For where two or three have gathered together in My name, I am there in their midst. Matthew 18:20-21

A great deal of thanks goes to all who took my manuscript and fine-tuned it with their excellent editing skills, Biblical insights, and wise suggestions. In their different ways, each made this book better than what it would have been without their contribution.

These special friends and family members include Myrna, Linus, Don, Keith, Ralph, Catherine, Rick, Brodie, Paul, Gilbert, and Jim.

Copyright 2019 Kent McClain
Web site -www.tmoments.com
Published by *Destinee Media* (March 2019)
Cover design: Myrna Winnian Sleath

Other books by Kent McClain

Teachable Moments
(Teaching Children How to Remember God's Truth)

Sowing Teachable Moments
(Memorable and Interactive Lessons to help Children Remember God's Truth)

What Was I Thinking?
(Learning an Ocean of Grace in a Pond of Legalism)

Mission Possible
(The Sequence of How Jesus Discipled the 12)
Currently out of print

Table of Contents

Homosexuality, Transgender People, and the Scriptures	Chapter 1
Born Homosexual	Chapter 2
"Coming out"	Chapter 3
Homophobia	Chapter 4
Worse Than Other Sins	Chapter 5
Jesus and Gays	Chapter 6
God's Judgment and Sexual Disease	Chapter 7
Christians Who Adopt the Gay Lifestyle or Change Gender	Chapter 8
Judging the LGBT Community	Chapter 9
Churches that Validate the LGBT Agenda	Chapter 10
Government Leaders, Justices, and Educators that Legislate for the LGBT agenda	Chapter 11
Hollywood and the Media's Push	Chapter 12
Reaching Out and Loving the LGBT Community	Chapter 13
Conclusion (Last questions)	Chapter 14
Questions from the Chapters	Appendix

Introduction

Wisdom from God is pure, peaceable, gentle, reasonable, and full of mercy. His words are unwavering, without hypocrisy, active, and sharper than any two-edged sword, which is able to pierce the soul and spirit. James 3:17; Hebrews 4:12-13 (RBK)

This book and the questions within are earmarked toward Christians, so they will have a better grasp on how to minister to those who identify themselves as homosexual or align with the LGBT Community.

I find the subjects of homosexuality and gender change to be two of the most controversial and challenging on which I have written. This was not the case in 2001 when I first wrote about homosexuality and one of its derivatives, same-sex marriage. When I presented a Biblical view of homosexuality and same-sex marriage back then, I received a lot of agreement, encouragement, and supportive comments from other Christians. Some of those comments are still on my website at www.tmoments.com.

This has not been the case this time around. American culture has changed and now reacts with greater tolerance towards all spinoffs of homosexuality, including gender change, which was hardly on the radar back in 2001. Several Christians have cautioned and even encouraged me to reconsider writing on this subject, as I may get heavily criticized, harassed, or ridiculed. Nevertheless, I have forged ahead and written a book that focuses on what the Scriptures teach about homosexuality, gender change, and their derivatives.

This book explores many difficult questions about this issue, some are rhetorical, but most are not. These are listed in the appendix at the back of the book according to where they occur. The answers to these questions are based on Scripture and my experiences or conversations with gays and those who have changed their gender. Some were friends, acquaintances, and others participated in some of my previous ministries. In case you were wondering, I have never been gay or interested in changing my sex. I have different temptations, desires, and enticements in this life, but these are not among them.

I have noted in this work a significant divide among churches today on ways to minister to gays and the transgender person. On one end of the spectrum, some churches feel we must accept homosexuals and the transgender person as is, and not try to change them. Other churches reject and refuse to minister to those who have these sexual orientations and lifestyles. Both church philosophies have elements of rightness and wrongness in their approach to applying what they believe God would have them do according to the Scriptures.

Special notes regarding terminology

The following terms: homosexual, gay, and LGBT will be used interchangeably throughout the book. Homosexual is the term the Bible uses to describe a sexual relationship or attraction between those of the same gender. Gay means the same but is a more acceptable term in many societies and cultures today. The acronym LGBT (Lesbian, Gay, Bisexual, and Transgender) stands for different expressions of homosexuality and gender identity.

L-**Lesbian** is a female homosexual, one who experiences romantic love or sexual attraction to other females.
G-**Gay** is often used to describe homosexual males but can also be applied to homosexual females.
B-**Bisexual** identifies both males and females who have romantic and sexual desire toward both genders.
T-**Transgender person** is one who has chosen a gender identity that does not correspond to his or her birth sex. A transsexual is a transgender person who has undergone a medical procedure to make a gender change.

Besides homosexual, other terms found in Scripture that relate to homosexuality include effeminate and cross-dressing.

Effeminate- A boy or man who intentionally tries to display feminine traits, so he can be identified as a woman. The opposite would also be true of a woman trying to become like a man. Both are forerunners to changing one's gender. There are those who may naturally display traits of the opposite sex, but this does not condemn them. It is only when they try and be the opposite gender that puts them in opposition to God and His design for them.

Cross-dressing- To dress in clothing that is usually worn by the opposite gender with the intent to be identified with that gender. This is yet another precursor associated with changing one's gender.

The terms **Scripture, Scriptures, Bible, Word,** and **Word of God** are all the same and will be used throughout interchangeably.

When using the term *Hollywood*, I am not referring to a particular city or even the people who live in this Southern California metropolitan area, but to those who make up the news media and entertainment business. In a broad sense, 'Hollywood" in this book also refers to those who are deemed *worldly*, that is, those whose lifestyles run counter to God and His written Word.

The initials RBK, which may come after a particular quoted Scripture, stands for **r**evised **b**y **K**ent, the author. I revised some verses for the sake of brevity. In the process of doing this, I worked hard to make sure the original meaning of these verses was not changed.

The quoted passages and verses within the text are usually from the New American Standard (NASB) Version.

This chapter is based on 4 verses in 2 passages of Scripture

This book is based on 507 verses in 187 passages of Scripture (Some verses are repeated in certain chapters)

Chapter 1

Homosexuality, Transgender People, and the Scriptures

What does the Bible teach about homosexuality and transgender people?

> *Thy Word is a lamp to my feet and a light to my path. All Scripture is inspired by God and profitable for teaching, for reproof, for correction, for training in righteousness. Psalm 119:105 & II Timothy 3:16*

This chapter may seem a bit tough on the LGBT community, but irrespective of this, those in these communities need to be loved. In accomplishing this, revealing God's truth about what they are doing is a key part of expressing this love. Other parts include friendship, acceptance, grace, loving discipline, and forgiveness. These attributes will be discussed further in other chapters, which hopefully will give a complete picture of the love Christians are to have toward these individuals.

The following passages of Scripture, which claim to be inspired by God, reflect His view of homosexuality and all of its derivatives. These Scriptures may seem harsh, condemning, and even uncompassionate at times, yet each is necessary to get those struggling with these practices into His kingdom.

What specific passages mention or refer to homosexuality?

Nine key passages mention or refer to homosexuality. The most straightforward and validating are listed first. They appear in both the Old and New Testaments, five in the Old, and four in the New.

Passage 1-Leviticus 18:22-24

> [22] *You shall not lie with a male as one lies with a female; it is an abomination.* [23] *Also, you shall not have intercourse with any animal to be defiled with it, nor shall any woman stand before an animal to mate with it; it is a perversion.* [24] *Do not defile yourselves by any of these things; for by all these the nations which I am casting out before you have become defiled.*

***Comment*-** In this Old Testament passage homosexuality is condemned and is specially called an abomination. In other words, it is something that is very shameful and loathsome to God and His design. It is mentioned alongside another revolting and forbidden act: intercourse with an animal.

Passage 2-Leviticus 20:13

> *If there is a man who lies with a male as those who lie with a woman, both of them have committed a detestable act; they shall surely be put to death. Their bloodguiltiness is upon them.*

***Comment*-** In this Old Testament passage homosexuality is a detestable act that was worthy of death in Israel. Even though such a punishment is no longer employed by Israel, or in most countries, it does not take away God's condemnation of this sin.

Passage 3 I-Timothy 1:8-11

> [8] *But we know that the Law is good, if one uses it lawfully,* [9] *realizing the fact that law is not made for a righteous person, but for those who are lawless and rebellious, for the ungodly and sinners, for the unholy and profane, for those who kill their fathers or mothers, for the murderers* [10] *and immoral men and homosexuals and kidnappers and liars and perjurers, and whatever else is contrary to sound teaching,* [11] *according to the glorious gospel of the blessed God, with which I have been entrusted.*

***Comment*-** This New Testament passage was written by Paul, the one whom God called upon to explain more about God's grace, mercy, and forgiveness than possibly any other writer of the Bible. By the end of his life and ministry, Paul had composed almost half the books in the New Testament. In this particular passage, he identified homosexuals as unholy and profane along with murderers, immoral men, kidnappers, liars, and perjurers.

Passage 4-I Corinthians 6:9-11

> [9] *Or do you not know that the unrighteous will not inherit the kingdom of God? Do not be deceived; neither fornicators, nor*

idolaters, nor adulterers, nor effeminate [a forerunner to gender change], nor homosexuals, [10] nor thieves, nor the covetous, nor drunkards, nor revilers, nor swindlers, will inherit the kingdom of God. [11] Such were some of you, but you were washed, but you were sanctified, but you were justified in the name of the Lord Jesus Christ and in the Spirit of our God.

Comment- In this letter to the church in Corinth, Paul warns that those who commit homosexuality are unrighteous and unfit for the kingdom, as were fornicators, idolaters, adulterers, the effeminate, thieves, coveters, drunkards, revilers, and swindlers. Quite a list with which to be grouped, wouldn't you say?

According to Paul, an unrepentant response or unbelieving heart in respect to a sin like this, or any other as far as that is concerned, would disqualify one from entering the kingdom of God. This means exclusion from salvation, exclusion from an abiding relationship with God, and exclusion from a heavenly reward.

But because of your stubbornness and your unrepentant heart, you are storing up wrath against yourself for the day of God's wrath, when his righteous judgment will be revealed. Romans 2:5

Passage 5-Romans 1:20-32

[20] For since the creation of the world His invisible attributes, His eternal power, and divine nature, have been clearly seen, being understood through what has been made, so that they are without excuse. [21] For even though they knew God, they did not honor Him as God or give thanks, but they became futile in their speculations, and their foolish heart was darkened. [22] Professing to be wise, they became fools, [23] and exchanged the glory of the incorruptible God for an image in the form of corruptible man and of birds and four-footed animals and crawling creatures. [24] Therefore God gave them over in the lusts of their hearts to impurity, so that their bodies would be dishonored among them. [25] For they exchanged the truth of God for a lie and worshiped and served the creature rather than the Creator, who is blessed forever. Amen. [26] For this reason God gave them over to degrading passions; for their women exchanged the natural function for that which is unnatural, [27] and in the same way also the men abandoned the natural

function of the woman and burned in their desire toward one another, men with men committing indecent acts and receiving in their own persons the due penalty of their error ^{28} *And just as they did not see fit to acknowledge God any longer, God gave them over to a depraved mind, to do those things which are not proper,* ^{29} *being filled with all unrighteousness, wickedness, greed, evil; full of envy, murder, strife, deceit, malice; they are gossips, 30 slanderers, haters of God, insolent, arrogant, boastful, inventors of evil, disobedient to parents,* ^{31}*without understanding, untrustworthy, unloving, unmerciful;* ^{32} *and although they know the ordinance of God, that those who practice such things are worthy of death, they not only do the same but also give hearty approval to those who practice them.*

Comment- Paul is very explicit here about homosexuality, showing the heart can spiral away from honoring God and His design. The foolish heart tries to reverse its own nature where men end up sexually attracted to men and women to women which is worthy of death.

As this passage closes, Paul again groups homosexuality with other detestable sins. This doesn't mean those who claim to be gay commit all the other sins recorded here, but it does mean that homosexuality is no less sinful than the ones cited. These include reprobates, murderers, backbiters, covenant breakers, inventors of evil, haters of God, and being deceitful, insolent, malicious, covetous, disobedient, haughty, boastful, unmerciful, absent of natural affection, and full of envy.

Passage 6-Genesis 19:1; 4-7; 10-13; 24-25

^{1}*Now the two angels came to Sodom in the evening as Lot was sitting in the gate of Sodom. When Lot saw them, he rose to meet them and bowed down with his face to the ground.* ^{4}*Before they lay down, the men of the city, the men of Sodom, surrounded the house, both young and old, all the people from every quarter;* ^{5}*and they called to Lot and said to him, "Where are the men who came to you tonight? Bring them out to us that we may have relations with them."* ^{6}*But Lot went out to them at the doorway, and shut the door behind him,* ^{7}*and said, "Please, my brothers, do not act wickedly."* ^{10}*But the men reached out their hands and brought Lot into the house with them, and shut the door.* ^{11}*They struck the men* *who were at the doorway of the house with blindness, both small and great so that they wearied themselves trying to find the doorway." ^{12}Then the two men said to Lot, "Whom else have you here? A son-in-law, and your sons, and your daughters, and whomever you have in the city bring them out of the place; ^{13}for we are about to destroy this place because their outcry has become so great before the Lord that the Lord has sent us to destroy it." ^{24}Then the Lord rained on Sodom, and Gomorrah brimstone and fire from the Lord out of heaven, ^{25}and He overthrew those cities, and the entire valley, and all the inhabitants of the cities, and what grew on the ground.*

Comment- This passage tells of an event in the Old Testament where men from every quadrant of the city of Sodom, young and old, showed up at Lot's door one night demanding to have sex with the two men visiting him. The two visitors, though, were not men, but angels. They had come to rescue Lot and his family from impending doom. Sodom along with nearby Gomorrah was going to be destroyed because of their exceeding wickedness.

It cannot be ignored that homosexual lust and behavior in this account was highlighted as perhaps one of the greatest of sins in Sodom. So, God destroyed Sodom and Gomorrah because of their many sins, including the sin of homosexuality.

Passage 7-Judges 19:22-23
^{22}While they were celebrating, behold, the men of the city, certain worthless fellows, surrounded the house, pounding the door; and they spoke to the owner of the house, the old man, saying, "Bring out the man who came into your house that we may have relations with him." ^{23}Then the man, the owner of the house, went out to them and said to them, "No, my fellows, please do not act so wickedly; since this man has come into my house, do not commit this act of folly."

Comment- In this passage, homosexuality was deemed wicked and an act of folly. Because it was not dealt with according to Leviticus 18 and 20, one event led to another which in turn led to the tribe of Benjamin being all but wiped out by the rest of Israel. The resulting event, however, is not the point; the point is that homosexuality was identified as wicked and full of folly.

Passage 8-Jude 6-7

⁶And the angels who did not stay within their own position of authority, but left their proper dwelling, He (God) kept them in eternal chains under gloomy darkness until the judgment of the great day, ⁷just as Sodom and Gomorrah and the surrounding cities, which likewise indulged in sexual immorality and pursued unnatural (strange) desires, serve as an example by undergoing a punishment of eternal fire. (English Standard Version & RBK)

Comment- In respect to homosexuality, Jude recorded that the final judgment of the angels who had rebelled against God would be like the destruction of Sodom and Gomorrah. And, like Sodom and Gomorrah, the sin of these fallen angels involved unnatural sex. As previously stated, unnatural sex was deemed immoral and associated with being wicked and rebellious. *(See Romans 1:26-27 above.)*

What specific passages allude to gender change?

Along with Deuteronomy 22:5, I Corinthians 6:9 plays a complementary role in explaining the development of gender change through the Scriptures. I Corinthians 6:9 has already been referred to in passage 4, which brought out another condemning point about homosexuality.

Deuteronomy 22:5
A woman shall not wear man's clothing, nor shall a man put on a woman's clothing; for whoever does these things is an abomination to the Lord your God. [Forerunner to gender change]

I Corinthians 6:9
⁹Do you not know that the unrighteous will not inherit the kingdom of God? Do not be deceived...the effeminate... will not inherit the kingdom of God. [Forerunner to gender change] (RBK)

Comment- In the Deuteronomy passage, Israelites were condemned for deliberately dressing or acting opposite of the sex to which they were born. Such an act was an abomination to God because, in essence, it was like telling Him that He didn't know what He was doing when creating a man to be a man or a woman, a woman. This was expressed in the Old Testament by cross-dressing, but, today, it has advanced to changing gender.

In the Corinthian passage, effeminacy is also condemned, because it carries with it the same idea of striving to be or act like the opposite sex. This is why it is a forerunner to changing gender in today'society because it rejects the sexual identity given to each of us by God at birth.

Effeminacy typically refers to a boy or man purposely acting or speaking like a woman, but the same could be applied to a woman trying to be like a man. The key, in either case, is the intent. If there is no intent or desire to be the opposite gender, then there is no reason to be overly concerned about one's level of feminine or masculine characteristics.

Last Thoughts

The great importance and role Scripture plays in this book with the issues of homosexuality and gender change, can be seen in the following quote by Priscilla Howe:

> *The Bible is a book that contains the mind of God, the state of man, the way of salvation, the fate of sinners, and the joy promised to all believers. Its doctrines are right, precepts binding, histories true, and decisions irrefutable. The Scriptures contain the light needed to direct our paths and the spiritual food to support, comfort and cheer our hearts. It is a traveler's map, a pilgrim's staff, a soldier's sword, and a Christian's charter. In it paradise is revealed, heaven opened up, and the realities of loss and hell disclosed. Christ is its grand focus, and our salvation is one of its most important aims. The Scriptures can fill our minds with truth, rule our hearts, and guide our steps.* [1]

The Bible is God's inspired and written Word on just about every subject in this life including homosexuality and gender change. Whether a man tries to be or act like a woman or a woman like a man, this very attempt says to God that He was mistaken when making some of us the way He did. God does not make any mistakes in His human design; it is we who make the mistake of trying to change or alter what He has done.

For the word of God is living and active and sharper than any two-edged sword, and piercing as far as the division of soul and spirit, of both joints and marrow, and able to judge the thoughts and intentions of the heart. Hebrew 4:12

This chapter is based on 42 verses in 10 passages of Scripture

Footnotes

1. Mrs. Charles Cowman, *Streams in the Desert Volume II* (Grand Rapids, Michigan, Zondervan Publishing House, 1966), October 15th devotional. (Also, revised and words added by Kent McClain)

Chapter 2

Born Homosexual

Can a person be born or destined to be homosexual?

Surely I was sinful at birth, sinful from the time my mother conceived me. Psalm 51:5 (RBK)

Can a person be born or destined by God to be homosexual? No, not really, according to the Scriptures. No one, no matter what they believe about themselves or others, is designed or intended by God to be anything but a man or a woman He created with the normal desires of a man or woman. To think or live otherwise is to be in rebellion against His will and purpose. There are no exceptions with the God of the Bible: a man is to live his life as a man in all respects, and a woman is to do the same with her life. This not only applies to those who claim homosexuality, but also to those who try and change their gender.

To be made in the image of God, which we are according to God's written revelation, includes acknowledging and respecting the sexual identity He gave to each one of us at birth. *(Genesis 1:27)* The Lord did not make any mistakes when He created us. What He did was well thought out and planned from the very beginning of man's creation even before we were born. *(Psalm 139:15)*

If there is confusion on the matter, it comes from the distortions and ideologies of culture, and the sin nature we all inherited at birth. This sin nature, His Word tells us, can express itself in many different ways; homosexuality and gender change are simply two of those. *(See I Corinthians 6:9-11 and I Timothy 1:8-10 in Chapter 1).*

The following are some Scriptures that tell us of the birth and continuing presence of our sin nature.

We were by nature children of wrath, even as the rest. Ephesians 2:3

For the intent of man's heart is evil from his youth. Genesis 8:20

> *Knowing this, that our old self was crucified with Him, in order that our body of sin might be done away with so that we would no longer be slaves to sin. Romans 6:6*
>
> *In reference to your former manner of life, you lay aside the old self, which is being corrupted in accordance with the lusts of deceit, and that you be renewed in the spirit of your mind, and put on the new self, which in the likeness of God has been created in righteousness and holiness of the truth. Ephesians 4:22-24*
>
> *For I know that nothing good dwells in me, that is, in my flesh; for the willing is present in me, but the doing of the good is not. For the good that I want, I do not do, but I practice the very evil that I do not want. But if I am doing the very thing I do not want, I am no longer the one doing it, but sin which dwells in me. I find then the principle that evil is present in me, the one who wants to do good. Wretched man that I am! Who will set me free from the body of this death? Thanks be to God through Jesus Christ our Lord! Romans 7:18-25*

Those who believe they are born gay or with a desire to change their gender are both deceived and wrong. Everyone is born with a sin nature and from that nature comes a variety of sins. One set of sins may tempt and take down one person, but not another. We often cringe at those who commit acts of homosexuality or gender change while being just as guilty of sins considered more acceptable. The good news is that all sin, no matter what it is, can be erased if we repent and ask Christ into our hearts. After doing this, we have the power of the Holy Spirit to overcome these sins including homosexuality.

Therefore, to say we were born gay or of the wrong gender is like saying, "we were born to be an adulterer, murderer, thief, or swindler" because these offenses all run together with homosexuality in the same Scriptural grouping. In fact, according to I Corinthians 6 and I Timothy 1, mentioned in Chapter 1, homosexuality and effeminacy [forerunner to gender change) both fall right in the middle of the pact of these wrongdoings.

Homosexuality or changing one's gender is therefore not a gray area in the Bible or on the proverbial bubble, so to speak. With God, these are hardcore sins that He has rejected from the beginning of time. They are distortions of God's design and will keep us from having a relationship with Him, for His Word says they are detestable. *(See Leviticus 20:13 in Chapter 1)*

Last Thoughts

With the truth in view about being born with a sin nature, rather than a homosexual or gender changing nature, how should we treat those who still believe this about themselves?

The short answer is we must love and seek them out as Jesus did with sinners of His day. Jesus did not hesitate to spend time with sinners. He talked and ate with them, and even healed some on occasion to bring about faith. (*Mark 5:2-8*) Yet, in the midst of Jesus building relationships with those who were sinning, He also was forthright in telling them the truth about their sins. He never played down their transgressions, nor indicated what they did was right. He did not hesitate to bring up past sins as with the woman at the well, but He gave hope of forgiveness and transformation. *(John 4:10, 13-18, 25-26, 28-30, 39-42)*

As we minister to those who are committing sins like homosexuality or who have changed their sex, we must treat them as Jesus did: spend time, care for them, lead them to Him for salvation, and teach them the truth about what they are doing. They may hate us at first for questioning their practices and lifestyles, but to truly love them as Christ did means we must be open and honest with them about everything.

Scripture References

Genesis 1:27 *God created man in His own image, in the image of God. He created him; male and female He created them.*

Psalm 139:15 *My frame was not hidden from You when I was made in secret, and skillfully wrought in the depths of the earth.*

Mark 5:2-8 *²When He got out of the boat, immediately a man from the tombs with an unclean spirit met Him, ³and he had his dwelling among the tombs. And no one was able to bind him anymore, even with a chain; ⁴because he had often been bound with shackles and chains, and the chains had been torn apart by him and the shackles broken in pieces, and no one was strong enough to subdue him. ⁵Constantly, night and day, he* *was screaming among the tombs and in the mountains, and gashing himself with stones. ⁶Seeing Jesus from a distance, he ran up and bowed down before Him; ⁷and shouting with a loud voice, he said, "What business do we have with each other, Jesus, Son of the Most High God? I implore You by God, do not torment me!' ⁸For He had been saying to him, 'Come out of the man, you unclean spirit!"*

John 4:10, 13-19, 25-26, 28-30, 39-42 *¹⁰Jesus answered and said to her, "If you knew the gift of God, and who it is who says to you, Give Me a drink, you would have asked Him, and He would have given you living water." ¹³Jesus answered and said to her, "Everyone who drinks of this water will thirst again; ¹⁴but whoever drinks of the water that I will give him shall never thirst, but the water that I will give him will become in him a well of water springing up to eternal life." ¹⁵The woman said to Him, "Sir, give me this water, so I will not be thirsty nor come all the way here to draw." ¹⁶He said to her, "Go, call your husband and come here." ¹⁷The woman answered and said, "I have no husband." Jesus said to her, "You have correctly said, I have no husband; ¹⁸for you have had five husbands, and the one whom you now have is not your husband." ¹⁹The woman said to Him, "Sir, I perceive that You are a prophet. ²⁵The woman said to Him, "I know that Messiah is coming (He who is called Christ); when that One comes, He will declare all things to us." ²⁶Jesus said to her, "I who speak to you am He." ²⁸So the woman left her water pot, and went into the city and said to the men, ²⁹ "Come, see a man who told me all the things that I have done; this is not the Christ, is it?" ³⁰They went out of the city and were coming to Him. ³⁹From that city many of the Samaritans believed in Him because of the word of the woman who testified, He told me all the things that I have done. ⁴⁰So when the Samaritans came to Jesus, they were asking Him to stay with them; and He stayed there two days. ⁴¹Many more believed because of His word; ⁴ and they were saying to the woman, "It is no longer because of what you said that we believe, for we have heard for ourselves and knew that this One is indeed the Savior of the world."*

This chapter is based on 45 verses in 13 passages of Scripture

Chapter 3

"Coming out"

What is the reality of someone "coming out" about their homosexuality or gender change?

> *There is a way of a man that is foolish, a way that seems right to him, and there are those who even approve of his words, ... but in the end, it all leads to death. Psalm 49:13 & Proverbs 16:25*

    The phrase "coming out", by consensus, is openly admitting to others that one is gay or at least has homosexual leanings, feelings, or desires. Such a "coming out" admittance is more and more celebrated in American society today and now lauded as an act of bravery. It is like being proud to be identified as a teacher, doctor, soldier, athlete, civil servant, businessman or religious leader. This is true now for those claiming to be gay. To speak out against those who claim this new identity, even though the Bible strongly warns against such a lifestyle, puts those who support God's Word on this issue at risk. The amount of risk depends upon where one lives. If we reside in a big city in a liberal state, the risk can be great. The risk is not as great for those who live in more conservative areas of the country.
    Whether we like it or not, Christian values and standards which once permeated America have gradually been discarded by those currently in control of the government, courts, large businesses, and public-school systems. Add to this the continual demeaning that the entertainment and media industries have exacted on our values and standards, and we can rightfully conclude that in the years to come most Christian morality will mirror the world. If this happens then, according to the Scriptures, America will be viewed by God as a lawless and rebellious nation without any sense of His morality. This would be catastrophic as in the past when God abandoned nations who became ungodly after once believing. For example, Israel, in the Old Testament, came close to losing its entire nation twice due to its lack of faithfulness to God and His principles.

> *Yet you have not listened to Me declares the Lord in order that you might provoke Me to anger with the work of your hands to your*

own harm. Therefore, thus says the Lord, because you have not obeyed My words, I will take all the families and send them to Nebuchadnezzar king of Babylon, this whole land will be a desolation and a horror, and will serve the king of Babylon seventy years (Jeremiah 25:7-11 RBK)

Regardless of what the American value system becomes, practices like homosexuality and changing one's gender have and will always dishonor God. It is not something He said was bad in a previous era, but okay today. If that were the case, then God would have amended such an important transition somewhere in Scripture. He did amend other practices like the food laws of the Old and New Testaments (*Leviticus 11:4, 7; Acts 10:9-15*). Homosexuality, however, is condemned in both the Old and New Testament, from Genesis to Revelation. *(In the Old Testament era - see Leviticus 20:13 and Deuteronomy 22:5 in Chapter 1. In the current New Testament era - see Romans 1:22, 24, 26, 27 and I Timothy 1:9-11 in Chapter 1)*

Therefore, "coming out" as being gay, effeminate, a cross-dresser, a transgender person, or a partner in a same-sex marriage brings greater warnings and judgments from God. "Coming out" is like saying to Him, "I don't care what is revealed in Scripture, I will openly and proudly live my gay life, and tell others to do likewise."

Why are there no apparent feelings of guilt for those who say this when guilt is attached to sin according to the Scripture? *(Ezra 9:7; Romans 3:23; James 2:10)*

The Lord uses or allows guilt not so much to punish those who are sinning but getting them to change their hearts and minds toward what they are doing. Not everyone feels the same amount of guilt when they sin against God or His teachings. Some, for instance, feel more guilt because they are closer to Him. Hopefully, the guilt they feel will lead to belief, repentance, and change which is His desire for them. Others feel less guilt because God is far off from their thoughts and plans in this life. This doesn't mean, though, there is no guilt associated with what they are doing or have done; it just means they have effectively rationalized it and shoved it under the rug. Perhaps only at death, will they realize the magnitude of the guilt they've accumulated as they stand before God, face to face. The tragedy at this point is there is nothing they can do about their guilt, for it will indict and keep them out of God's kingdom forever.

In addition to shoving guilt under the rug, there is another reason why gays, in particular, feel free and liberated when they "come out" about their homosexuality. It is because when anyone hides something for a long time, whether good or bad, and then finally confesses or exposes it, the usual result is relief and joy, at first. This reaction is just a part of the sin nature we all have, which generates a variety of false feelings and assurances. The immediate relief and joy from those who "come out," is only a temporary elation that will eventually pass, whether they admit it or not. By personal experience, not with homosexuality, but with other sins I've committed, if sin is not dealt with through confession and receiving God's forgiveness, then guilt continues, increases, and even worsens over time. As the following Psalm teaches, the guilt God gives when we sin will emotionally and physically eat away at us.

> *When I kept silent about my sin, my body wasted away through my groaning all day long. For day and night, Your hand was heavy upon me; my vitality was drained away as with the fever heat of summer. I acknowledged my sin to You, and my iniquity I did not hide. I said, "I will confess my transgressions to the Lord", and You forgave the guilt of my sin. Psalm 32:3-5*

Gays and those who change their gender often open up about their lifestyles because they want the company and acceptance of others. There is an adage that "misery loves company". Gays and those who change their gender not only need the company of others for fellowship and acceptance but also to validate what they are doing. If by "coming out", they can get a large and important following, this makes it seem like what they are doing is not so wrong, and even "right." Nevertheless, the Bible remains very consistent and solid on homosexuality: it is wrong and is considered detestable, an abomination, and a perversion in God's eyes. *(See Leviticus 18:22-24 in Chapter 1)*

Last Thoughts

How should we as Christians relate or minister to someone who has "come out" about their homosexuality or gender change? When someone openly admits this, I suggest we don't try and come up with a complete Biblical perspective and solution right away, but rather thank them for sharing their revelation. Build a relationship with them before giving any Biblical answers or advice. If they are already a friend, don't turn away from them because of the choice they've made. Instead, continue to listen to them, and even ask how they came to that conclusion. Let them talk about their feelings. If one session is not enough, then arrange for another. At the end of each conversation, make every effort to end with prayer, as this directly brings God into the conversation.

If they want to know how we feel about them being a transgender or gay person, then share what the Bible says about their practice or lifestyle. As you do, be kind, but don't water down the Scriptures in the process. Let the Word speak to your friend. *(Hebrews 4:12)* The Word of God does not return void.

If we ever feel uncomfortable with them in our conversations, then ask another Christian to join in. If possible, choose someone who has gone through what they are now going through, but has turned to Christ. If they don't want someone else to join in, then I suggest not meeting with them for a while. Sometimes those committing sexual sins like homosexuality have another agenda in mind when confidentially sharing about it. They may be seeking to recruit one to their viewpoint or lifestyle.

Can those who openly proclaim themselves homosexual or embrace any other derivative of it enter the kingdom of God? It all depends upon what is really in their hearts when they "come out." In the end, only God can judge the heart and whether a person truly believes or will believe in the future. According to Scripture, if they want to have a relationship with God, but refuse to repent of their sinful lifestyles, then they will not be allowed into His kingdom. Even so, God has an endless ocean of acceptance and forgiveness available to all in the LGBT Community. Yet, He will not take any into His kingdom on their own terms, unless they put their trust in Him and ask forgiveness for all of their sins. *(See I Corinthians 6: 9-11 in Chapter 1)*

If we believe and ask God to forgive us of our sins, but then revert to some of them, will we still remain in His kingdom? The answer is yes. God promises never to leave nor forsake us, no matter what. In addition to this promise, God also gives us the Spirit to daily help us conquer old sinful habits and lifestyles. He never gives up on us. But we must not quench or grieve the Spirit, or we will end up like the person who survived a fire but lost everything else in the process.

> *Now if any man builds on the foundation with gold, silver, precious stones, wood, hay, straw, each man's work will become evident; for the day will show it because it is to be revealed with fire, and the fire itself will test the quality of each man's work. If any man's work which he has built on it remains, he will receive a reward. If any man's work is burned up, he will suffer loss; but he himself will be saved, yet so as through fire. I Corinthians 3:12-15*

Scripture References

Leviticus 11:4,7. *[4]Nevertheless these you shall not eat...[7]the swine, though it divides the hoof, having cloven hooves, yet does not chew the cud, is unclean to you.*

Acts 10: 9-15 *[9]On the next day, as they were on their way and approaching the city, Peter went up on the housetop about the sixth hour to pray. [10]But he became hungry and was desiring to eat; but while they were making preparations, he fell into a trance;[11]and he beheld the sky opened up, and a certain object like a great sheet coming down, lowered by four corners to the ground, [12]and there were in it all kinds of four-footed animals and crawling creatures of the earth and birds of the air. [13]A voice came to him, "Get up, Peter, kill and eat!" [14]But Peter said, "By no means, Lord, for I have never eaten anything unholy and unclean." [15]Again a voice came to him a second time, "What God has cleansed, no longer consider unholy."*

Ezra 9:7 *Since the days of our fathers to this day we have been in great guilt, and on account of our iniquities.*

Romans 3:23 *For all have sinned and fall short of the glory of God.*

James 2:10 *For whoever keeps the whole law and yet stumbles in one point, he has become guilty of all.*

Hebrews 4:12 *For the word of God is living and active and sharper than any two-edged sword and piercing as far as the division of soul and spirit, of both joints and marrow, and able to judge the thoughts and intentions of the heart.*

This chapter is based on 35 verses in 13 passages of Scripture

Chapter 4

Homophobia

Are Christians homophobic, discriminators, racists or bigots in respect to the LGBT Community?

> *Blessed are you when people insult you and persecute you, and falsely say all kinds of evil against you because of Me. Rejoice and be glad, for your reward in heaven is great; for in the same way, they persecuted the prophets who were before you. Matthew 5:11-12*

Years ago, at the University of Wyoming, I taught my students tactics on how to win a debate. I told them if they felt they were beginning to lose the match, to attack their opponent's trustworthiness and credibility. In a debate, this is called an *ad hominem* argument (an argument or reaction directed against a person rather than the position they are supporting). Sometimes the tactic worked, and at other times it didn't, depending upon how articulate and merciless the attacking student might have been.

In the current debate over the practices of the LGBT Community in America, I have found those who either lack belief in God or who reinterpret what the Scriptures teach about these practices often use *ad hominem* arguments to win over others. They revert to calling Christians homophobic, discriminatory, prejudiced, racists, and even bigots. In addition to this name-calling, they sometimes go beyond winning others to their side and try and destroy Christian beliefs in the process. Regrettably, they have been successful to a degree, removing the Bible and prayer out of our public schools, and winning battles over abortion, same-sex marriage, euthanasia, mercy killing, and the use of social marijuana.

What's next for this ever-growing anti-Christian agenda? Perhaps, to push for the right to marry more than one partner at a time, or even to marry a same-sex mate and an opposite-sex mate at the same time. Maybe, and even worse than this, would be a future requirement that all religion-based institutions (schools, churches, synagogues, and Christian organizations) hire homosexuals and transgender people to their staff.

Regardless of what may happen, at the moment, Christians are being called and labeled all kinds of ugly names because of what they believe about homosexuality, a belief condemned and recorded in Leviticus 20:13, I Corinthians 6:9-11, and Romans 1:25-27. See Chapter 1.

What does it mean to be homophobic? By definition, it identifies those who harbor an irrational hatred or fear of homosexuality. That's what any phobia is, a great hatred or fear of something. However, Christians are not homophobic, because if they attend themselves to the Scriptures as they should, they will demonstrate no hatred or fear at all toward the homosexual community, only a desire to see them saved or recovered from their sins.

Neither are Christians discriminators. By definition, discriminators are those who speak out and do ill to others they deem as inferior. A Christian, as described in the Scripture, should never have a superior feeling toward anyone, but rather be clothed with as much humility as possible.

When ministering to homosexuals or to those who have changed their gender, we as Christians, are not to have a sense of superior feelings toward them, but rather a sense of humility. We should see them as more important than ourselves as the Scriptures teach. The following two verses bear this out, one from Jesus and the other from the Apostle Paul.

But the greatest among you shall be your servant. Whoever exalts himself shall be humbled, and whoever humbles himself shall be exalted. (Jesus, Matthew 23:11-12)

To me, the very least of all saints (believers), this grace was given, to preach to the Gentiles (non-Christians) the unfathomable riches of Christ. (Paul, Ephesians 3:8)

Neither are Christians bigots as some critics claim. What is a bigot? One who not only has a general dislike and prejudice toward others but also has a deep hatred and intolerance of them. Sometimes that hatred and intolerance are carried out through violence. The Ku Klux Klan, for example, is far more than just prejudiced or discriminatory against blacks; they are bigots toward them. In the past, they not only denied the rights of black Americans in our society, but ridiculed, beat, and even murdered them because of their race. This has been and is still today evil and disgusting.

When Christians are called bigots because of their opposition to the sin of homosexuality, they, in essence, are being tagged as intolerant and hate-filled. Nothing could be farther from the truth, for God through the Scriptures teaches all Christians to love others and hate no one, no matter who they are or what they've done.

> *But I say to you who hear, "Love your enemies, do good to those who hate you, bless those who curse you, pray for those who mistreat you. Whoever hits you on the cheek, offer him the other also; and whoever takes away your coat, do not withhold your shirt from him either. Give to everyone who asks of you, and whoever takes away what is yours, do not demand it back. Treat others the same way you want them to treat you." Luke 6:27-32*

A huge part of this loving process is to do all that is possible to help those drowning in sins like homosexuality, by building a loving relationship with them. Then share with them the path we have personally taken when accepting Christ's offer of salvation. Does this sound like the actions of a bigot? I think not!

Opponents of Christians also declare us to be racist-like in beliefs and actions. They say our rejection of those in the LGBT community is the same as rejecting a particular race, color, or gender. This is not true, because according to the Scriptures living an LGBT lifestyle is not something anyone was predetermined to be or to do, but a choice made, and a very sinful one indeed. *(See Leviticus 18:22-24 and I Timothy 1:8-10 in Chapter 1)*

Last Thoughts

When Christians follow the Scriptures on homosexuality will they suffer discrimination and rejection for speaking out against these practices? Yes, because many of the most powerful in our government, schools, judicial branches, media, and entertainment industries today pressure other Americans to accept all LGBT practices. They also push to discard what Christians say, even though what we say is based on the Bible.

Unfortunately, many Americans are giving in to this pressure. What a change in thinking and direction for us as a nation, whose founding leaders like Patrick Henry and Supreme Court Justice John Jay to name a few, did not hesitate to integrate Christian beliefs and the Scriptures into what would be good, right, and normal for America.

> *"It cannot be emphasized too strongly or too often that this great nation was founded, not by religionists, but by Christians; not on religions, but on the gospel of Jesus Christ. For this very reason peoples of other faiths have been afforded asylum, prosperity, and freedom of worship here.*[1] *Patrick Henry*
>
> *The Bible ... is a book worth more than all the other books that were ever printed."*[2] *Patrick Henry*
>
> *"In forming and settling my belief relative to the doctrines of Christianity, I adopted no articles from creeds but such only as, on careful examination, I found to be confirmed by the Bible."*[3] *John Jay (1st Chief Justice of the U.S. Supreme Court)*

This chapter is based on 20 verses in 9 passages of Scripture

Footnotes

1. M. E. Bradford, *The Trumpet Voice of Freedom: Patrick Henry of Virginia* (Plymouth Rock Foundation, 1991), page iii.
2. William Wirt, *Sketches of the Life and Character of Patrick Henry* (Published by James Webster), page 402.
3. George Pellew, *John Jay (American Statesman Series),* page 360.

Chapter 5

Worse Than Other Sins

Is the practice of homosexuality and gender change worse than other sins in the Bible?

For the sin of the daughter of my people is greater than the sin of Sodom... You who delivered me to the hands of Pilate has the greater sin. Lamentations 4:6; John 19:11

Since homosexuality is declared a sin throughout the Scripture, is it worse than any other sin? Some contend it isn't, because a sin is a sin and all are equally wrong before God. This is true in one sense, in that each sin carries with it just as much condemnation as another when it comes to salvation. *(Romans 3:23; Romans 6:23; John 3:16-18)*

It is also true that not every sin is the same with God; some are more damaging than others as revealed in the Lamentations and John passages above. We see this is to be true even in our own life experiences here on earth, for someone like Adolph Hitler, who murdered millions, is considered a greater sinner than a petty thief who breaks into a house and steals. This is perhaps why God's laws of the Old Testament had varying degrees of consequences for different sins, because God saw some sins as worse than others. *(Exodus 21:22-25; 22:1)*

Simply put, some sins are worse to commit than others according to the Bible. Homosexuality and effeminacy [forerunner to gender change] are two of the more severe and abominable ones. According to the Old and New Testaments, homosexuality was worthy of a death penalty, which hardly makes it a *gray issue* as some contend within and outside of the church. *(See Leviticus 20:13, Deuteronomy 22:5, and Romans 1:26-28, 32 in Chapter 1)*

Homosexuality was not only considered conduct worthy of death, but it was also grouped together in the Scripture with other behaviors equally as offensive. The killing of a mother or father, the murder of another, and kidnapping are just a few offenses with which this practice is linked. In America today, homosexuals and transgender people are not associated with any of these behaviors, but they are in God's Word. *(See I Corinthians 6:9-11, I Timothy 1:8-10, and Romans 1:21-30 in Chapter 1)*

If we put together a catalog of sins and wrongdoings from I Corinthians 6:9-10, I Timothy 1:8-10, and Romans 1:21-30, most of the sins we commit as a society are listed. They include being a fornicator, idolater, adulterer, effeminate, homosexual, thief, drunkard, reviler, swindler, kidnapper, liar, perjurer, murderer, creator of strife, gossiper, slanderer, hater of God, inventor of evil, and a killer of parents. Also included are the sins of being untrustworthy, unloving, unmerciful, covetous, immoral, lawless, rebellious, ungodly, unholy, profane, unrighteous, wicked, greedy, evil, envious, deceitful, malicious, insolent, arrogant, and boastful. Quite a list for homosexuality to be grouped and associated with, wouldn't you say?

Last Thoughts

Why are homosexuality and changing gender sinful and rejected by God when these sexually-oriented behaviors seemingly don't harm anyone as other sins do? The Scripture does not directly answer this question. The answer I offer is based on what I perceive God's thinking was when He condemned these practices. I draw my conclusions from my study of the Scriptures, as well as a process of deductive reasoning.

First of all, God created both man and woman according to His own image; the genetics (XX or XY) of each were established at the time of conception. At birth, He also gave each gender very different physical frames, features, and roles to play in this world. For instance, the Lord gave men stronger bodies to take care of themselves and to provide safety for women and children.

Women, on the other hand, were given bodies that could bear children. *(Genesis 1:26 -27; I Peter 3:7)* If both men and women played their differing roles as God designed, then children would be born and bred in a safe, holistic, and protected environment. These children and their children, and their children's children would thus carry on God's kingdom on earth. This is the outcome of a man fulfilling his role as a man, and a woman as a woman. The point is that God created man to be different from a woman for a reason and purpose. Protection of the woman and childbearing are just two of many.

Nowhere in Scripture does it indicate that God mixed things up when creating a man to be a man and a woman a woman. He never created a man on the outside to be a woman on the inside or the reverse. To claim

He did, makes God out to be confused, disorganized, and not really God at all. Besides, if God did do this, then why would He call it a defilement and abominable act as He did in Leviticus 18:22-24 *(See Chapter 1)*

To conclude, are homosexuality, gender change, and their various offshoots worse sins than others? I believe they may be, according to the Scriptures, because not every sinful consequence is deserving of death. Homosexuality was at one time! And not every sin is grouped alongside being a murderer, hater of God, or inventor of evil. Homosexuality is according to Romans 1:21-30. *(See Chapter 1)*

Scriptural References

Romans 3:23 *For all have sinned and fell short of the glory of God.*

Romans 6:23 *For the wages of sin is death, but the free gift of God is eternal life in Christ Jesus our Lord.*

John 3:16-18 *^{16}For God so loved the world that he gave his only begotten Son, that whoever believeth in him should not perish, but have eternal life. ^{1} For God did not send the Son into the world to judge the world; but that the world should be saved through him. ^{18}He who believes in him is not judged; he who does not believe has been judged already because he has not believed in the name of the only begotten Son of God.*

Exodus 21:22-25 *^{22}And if men strive together and hurt a woman with child so that her fruit depart, and yet no harm follow; he shall be surely fined, according to as the woman's husband shall lay upon him, and he shall pay as the judges determine. ^{23}But if any harm follows, then thou shalt give life for life, ^{24} eye for an eye, tooth for tooth, hand for hand, foot for foot, ^{25}burning for burning, wound for wound, stripe for stripe.*

Exodus 22:1 *If a man shall steal an ox, or a sheep, and kill it, or sell it; he shall pay five oxen for an ox, and four sheep for a sheep.*

Genesis 1:26 -27 *^{26}And God said, Let us make man in our image, after our likeness: and let them have dominion over the fish of the sea, and over the birds of the heavens, and over the cattle, and over all the earth, and over every creeping thing that creeps upon the earth. ^{27}And God created man in* *his own image, in the image of God created him; male and female He created them.*

I Peter 3:7 *You husbands, in the same way, live with your wives in an understanding way, as with someone weaker, since she is a woman; and show her honor as a fellow heir of the grace of life, so that your prayers will not be hindered.*

This chapter is based on 39 verses in 16 passages of Scripture

Chapter 6

Jesus and Gays

How did Jesus view the homosexual issue?

What man among you, if he has a hundred sheep and has lost one of them, does he not leave the ninety-nine in the open pasture and go after the one which is lost until he finds it? When he has found it, he lays it on his shoulders, rejoicing. And when he comes home, he calls together his friends and his neighbors, saying to them, "Rejoice with me, for I have found my sheep which was lost! I tell you that in the same way, there will be more joy in heaven over one sinner who repents than over ninety-nine righteous persons who need no repentance." Luke 15:4-7

Jesus did not directly address gays, nor did He teach on the subject of homosexuality during his ministry on earth. But, He did address the issue of homosexuality, and its various practices before and after He came to earth. Associated practices of homosexuality in the first century included cross-dressers and the effeminate. Gender change would likely have been added to this mix had Jesus arrived in this century rather than the first. This is because each of these practices alters and perverts God's original design for the physical and psychological make-up of a man and a woman. *(Genesis 1:27, See Deuteronomy 22:5 and I Corinthians 6:9-10 in Chapter 1)*

It must be remembered that before Jesus came to earth, He existed as God himself along with God the Father and the Spirit. *(John 1:1-3, John 8:53-58)* As the Scripture teaches, Jesus is God, equal to the Father and Spirit in every way. Yet, in the midst of this, all three were also fully one God at the same time. *(John 10:30; Deuteronomy 6:4)*

This may be difficult to grasp because we have no human relationship on earth which compares. However, whether we fully understand the Trinity, Jesus was equally involved at the very beginning of time agreeing with God's pronouncements on homosexuality and gender change. He was also equally involved after His death and resurrection when Paul was inspired by the Spirit to write what he did about the practice of homosexuality. *(Romans 8:9-10)*

Therefore, on the one hand, Jesus never directly addressed gay issues while on earth, yet on the other hand, He did when He, the Father, and the Spirit inspired the Old and New Testaments. If you want to know more about how God the Father, Spirit, and Jesus work together, then I suggest checking out a book on Amazon.com that I have written entitled *Sowing Teachable Moments Year One*. Chapter 23 illustrates how the Father, Spirit, and Jesus are each God, as well as one God at the same time.

Jesus viewed gay practices as a sin that needed to be repented of, abandoned, and forgiven. These practices were not just common or run-of-the-mill-sins, but ones God the Father, God the Son, and God the Spirit considered and still considers today as abominable, detestable, and full of folly. Society's acceptance of these practices may seem like an advance in morality, but they are not according to Scriptures. They are just as sinful today in this New Testament era in which we live, as they were in Old Testament times. *(See Leviticus 18:22-24, Genesis 19:1-11, and Judges 19:22-23 in Chapter 1).*

Therefore, when coming to minister to us on earth, there was nothing for Jesus to change regarding homosexuality or gender change. What He, the Father, and the Spirit had determined about such a sin was set for all time. The laws and rules the Three (Trinity) established for the Jewish nation in this regard were never abolished nor annulled. Only the consequences changed when Jewish law was superseded by Roman law. The Jews came under the Roman law after being defeated by Rome, and under early Roman law, homosexuality was not illegal to practice, although it was generally looked down upon. [1]

> *Do not think that I came to abolish the Law or the Prophets; I did not come to abolish but to fulfill. For truly I say to you, until heaven and earth pass away, not the smallest letter or stroke shall pass from the Law until all is accomplished. Whoever then annuls one of the least of these commandments, and teaches others to do the same, shall be called least in the kingdom of heaven; but whoever keeps and teaches them, he shall be called great in the kingdom of heaven. Matthew 5:17-19*

Due to Israel's defeat as a nation and the spiritual ignorance they displayed when dealing with Jesus, the Son of God, their role as God's representative nation was suspended. Only during the end times will this suspension be lifted. *(Jeremiah 30:3)* Until that time, the church, which is led by the Spirit, takes over the role of being God's representative to the world. The church's emphasis is primarily on God's grace and forgiveness, rather than His laws. However, both are needed to give a complete picture of God's love, character, expectations, and will.

The church is made up of anyone and everyone who believes in Jesus as Lord and Savior, no matter the era, what part of the world they are from, station in life, or the culture of which they are apart. *(I Corinthians 12:12-14; Acts 28:20)*

It is, therefore, our responsibility as believers in the church to share Christ with everyone we can; to teach the truth about what is right and wrong according to the Scriptures; to emphasize God's grace and forgiveness, and to abide by the laws of our land when possible. Should any laws, including those that deal with homosexuality, demand from us something contrary to God's Word and our faith, then we are to be like Daniel of the Old Testament when he refused his government's edict to stop praying. His decision took him to the lion's den, but we know how that turned out. God may even do something similar for us if we stand against an issue like homosexuality. *(I Peter 2:13-14; Daniel 6:7-10)*

Should America's leaders continue to push for the acceptance of gay practices and gender change, then all we may be able to do is pray they change their minds and policies. While doing so and proclaiming the truth of the Scriptures, persecution and rejection may come. Sad to say, this is often the way it is when God's people stand up for His truth in this world. During such persecution, though, remember what the Christians were willing to endure under Nero's persecution, all for the sake of Christ and the Gospel.

Last Thoughts

During His ministry, Jesus modeled how to treat sinners which we all are. He taught sinners how to find salvation, how to understand the truth, and how to see their own sin for what it was. He also spent a great deal of time with as many sinners as possible. Jesus ate with sinners, walked and talked with sinners, and even associated with the most rejected and disgraced. He healed many, whether their faith was present or not. In the end, Jesus even gave up His life on the cross for their sins, no matter what they had done. *(Luke 7:39, 47-50; Luke 8:26-29; John 4:3-6, 8-11)*

We, as Christians, need to do the same with the gays and those changing their gender. They need to be ministered to as Jesus did with the sinners of His day. There is no doubt, according to Scripture, that homosexual sins of all kinds are abominable and detestable before God's eyes, but not too abominable or detestable for the sinner to be rescued.

Although we cannot sacrifice our own lives on a cross as Jesus did, we can love them as He did. This can be accomplished by spending time with them, helping them with their struggles, assisting them when they are sick, and being friends through thick and thin. At the same time, we should also teach them about their sins, and how God can forgive them for what they are doing to themselves and others. Hopefully, they will find salvation and freedom from their sins because of what we have done.

Scripture References

Genesis 1:27 *God created man in His own image, in the image of God He created him; male and female He created them.*

John 1:1-4 *¹In the beginning was the Word, and the Word was with God, and the Word was God. ²He was in the beginning with God. ³All things came into being through Him, and apart from Him, nothing came into being that has come into being. ⁴In Him was life, and the life was the Light of men.*

John 8:53-58 *⁵³Surely, you are not greater than our father Abraham, who died? The prophets died too; who do You make Yourself out to be? ⁵⁴Jesus answered, "If I glorify Myself, My glory is nothing; it is My Father who glorifies Me, of whom you say, He is our God; ⁵⁵and you have not come to know Him, but I know Him; and if I say that I do not know Him, I will be a liar like you, but I do know Him and keep His word. ⁵⁶Your father Abraham rejoiced to see My day, and he saw it and was glad." ⁵⁷So the Jews said to Him, "You are not yet fifty years old, and have You seen Abraham?" ⁵⁸Jesus said to them, "Truly, truly, I say to you, before Abraham was born, I am."*

John 10:30 *I and my Father are one.*

Deuteronomy 6:4 *Hear, O Israel: the Lord our God is one Lord.*

Romans 8:9-10 *⁹However, you are not in the flesh but in the Spirit, if indeed the Spirit of God dwells in you. But if anyone does not have the Spirit of Christ, he does not belong to Him. ¹⁰If Christ is in you, though the body is dead because of sin, yet the spirit is alive because of righteousness.*

Jeremiah 30:3 *For the time is coming when I will restore the fortunes of my people of Israel and Judah. I will bring them home to this land that I gave to their ancestors, and they will possess it and live here again. I, the Lord, have spoken!*

I Corinthians 12:12-14 *¹²For even as the body is one and yet have many members, and all the members of the body, though they are many, are one body, so also is Christ. ¹³For by one Spirit we were all baptized into one body, whether Jews or Greeks, whether slaves or free, and we were all made to drink of one Spirit. ¹⁴For the body is not one member, but many.*

Acts 20:28 *Be on guard for yourselves and for all the flock, among which the Holy Spirit has made you overseers, to shepherd the church of God which He purchased with His own blood.*

I Peter 2:13-14 *¹³Submit yourselves to every ordinance of man for the Lord's sake: whether it be to the king, as supreme; ¹⁴Or unto governors, as unto them are sent by him for the punishment of evildoers, and for the praise of them that do well.*

Daniel 6:7-10 *⁷All the commissioners of the kingdom, the prefects and the satraps, the high officials and the governors have consulted together that the king should establish a statute and enforce an injunction that anyone who makes a petition to any god or man beside you, "O king, for thirty days, shall be cast into the lion's den. ⁸Now, O king, establish the injunction and sign the document so that it may not be changed, according to the law of the Medes and Persians, which may not be revoked." ⁹Therefore King Darius signed the document, that is, the injunction. ¹⁰Now when Daniel knew that the document was signed, he entered his house (now in his roof chamber he had windows open toward Jerusalem); and* *he continued kneeling on his knees three times a day, praying and giving thanks before his God, as he had been doing previously.*

Luke 7:39; 47-50 *[39]Now when the Pharisee who had invited Him saw this, he said to himself, "If this man were a prophet He would know who and what sort of person this woman is who is touching Him, that she is a sinner."[47]For this reason, Jesus said to the Pharisee, "her sins, which are many, have been forgiven, for she loved much; but he who is forgiven little, loves little." [48]Then He said to her, "Your sins have been forgiven." [49]Those who were reclining at the table with Him began to say to themselves, "Who is this man who even forgives sins?" [50]And He said to the woman, "Your faith has saved you; go in peace." (RBK)*

Luke 8:26-29, 35-39 *[26]Then Jesus arrived in the country of the Gerasenes, which is opposite Galilee. [27]And when He came out onto the land, He was met by a man from the city who was possessed with demons. [28]And seeing Jesus, the demon-possessed man cried out and fell before Him, and said in a loud voice, "What business do we have with each other, Jesus, Son of the Most High God? I beg You, do not torment me" [29]Jesus then commanded the unclean spirit in the man to come out, for it had seized him many times. [35]The Gerasene people then went out to see what had happened; and they came to Jesus and found the man from whom the demons had gone out, sitting down at the feet of Jesus, clothed and in his right mind; and they became frightened. [36]Those who had seen this reported to others how the man who was demon-possessed had been made well. [37]Then all the people of the country of the Gerasenes and the surrounding district asked Him to leave them, for they were gripped with great fear; and He got into a boat and returned. [38]But the man from whom the demons had gone out was begging Him that he might accompany Him; but He sent him away, saying, [39]"Return to your house and describe what great things God has done for you." So, he went away, proclaiming throughout the whole city what great things Jesus had done for him." (RBK)*

John 4:46-47, 50-53 *[46]Therefore Jesus came again to Cana of Galilee, and there was a royal official whose son was sick at Capernaum. [47]He went to Christ and implored Him to come down and heal his son; for he was at the point of death. [50]Jesus said to him, "Go for your son lives." [51]*

As he was now going, his slaves met him, saying that his son was living. ⁵²So he inquired of them as to the hour when he began to get better. Then they said to him, "Yesterday at the seventh hour the fever left him." ⁵³So the father knew that it was at that hour in which Jesus said to him, "Your son lives." Then he and his whole household believed in Jesus. (RBK)

This chapter is based on 71 verses in 22 passages of Scripture

Footnotes

1. Robert Frakes, *Why the Romans Are Important in the Debate about Gay Marriage.* (https://historynewsnetwork.org/article/21319, February 19, 2006). *Side note,* Mr. Frakes taught in the History Department at Clarion University, 1991.

Chapter 7

God's Judgment and Sexual Disease

Is a sexual disease God's judgment against homosexuality?

Whatever a man sows, this he will also reap, for the one who sows to his own flesh will from the flesh reap corruption, but the one who sows to the Spirit will from the Spirit reap eternal life. Galatians 6:7-8

There is nothing in Scripture that indicates sexual disease or illness is God's earthly judgment on those practicing homosexuality. God's judgment only comes at the end of life, when we will all be evaluated according to our faith in Christ, and repentance of sins, no matter what they were or how many committed.

In as much as it is appointed for men to die once and after this comes judgment. Hebrews 9:27

For we must all appear before the judgment seat of Christ, so that each one may be recompensed for his deeds in the body, according to what he has done, whether good or bad. II Corinthians 5:10

Nevertheless, even though judgment is reserved for the end of our lives, this doesn't mean there won't be consequences, like a disease, for our behavior. For example, those who practice unprotected heterosexual sex with multiple partners may contract, as a consequence, various infections like venereal disease, gonorrhea (clap), syphilis, and herpes. Some, who practice homosexual or heterosexual sex with HIV infected partners, may catch the HIV virus (AIDS).

What are God's reasons for letting disease accompany sexual sin? Two reasons come to mind: the first is to get our attention about something wrong that we are doing. There is nothing like a disease, pain, or great discomfort to get our attention and God knows this.

A second reason is to get us to pray and depend on Him for help and salvation. Struggling with venereal disease, syphilis, herpes, or HIV can be very sobering and depressing, but it can also ignite within us a lot of soul-searching. If this soul-searching leads us into the kingdom of God, then what we had to go through was worth it. Living our lives goes far beyond this earthly existence; it is eternal, either with God or without Him.

As of this writing, HIV has claimed over 36 million lives worldwide, which is tragic. Hopefully many amongst those 36 million turned to God before they perished. Here are some Scriptures that possibly led them to put their faith and future with God.

> *If you confess with your mouth Jesus as Lord and believe in your heart that God raised Him from the dead, you will be saved; for with the heart a person believes, resulting in righteousness, and with the mouth, he confesses, resulting in salvation. Romans 10:9-10*

> *Do not let your heart be troubled; believe in God, also believe in Me. In My Father's house are many dwelling places; if it were not so, I would have told you; for I go to prepare a place for you. If I go and prepare a place for you, I will come again and receive you to Myself, that where I am, there you may be also. And you know the way where I am going. John 14:1-4*

Last Thoughts

Not everyone who contracts a sexual disease has sinned. Regrettably, there are innocent victims of other's sexual sins. There are those who have contracted the HIV virus via blood transfusions, and others who have contracted syphilis, gonorrhea, or herpes, because of an unfaithful husband or wife. I know of a mother of one of my past students who contracted AIDS because her husband had been unfaithful with another woman who had the HIV virus. The wife was devastated, to say the least, when she got HIV, although completely innocent.

Is this fair? No, it doesn't seem so. Yet, for God to give every person on earth the chance to choose right or wrong, there will always be innocent victims like this mother. Fortunately for her, she had a very strong relationship with Christ when this happened, which helped her greatly in living out the remainder of her life. She was never angry with God about this realizing He had a full life reserved for her in heaven.

I will give you the keys of the kingdom of heaven, and whatever you bind on earth shall have been bound in heaven, and whatever you loose on earth shall have been loosed in heaven. Matthew 16:19

This chapter is based on 10 verses in 5 passages of Scripture

Chapter 8

Christians Who Adopt the Homosexual Lifestyle or Change Gender

How should Christians minister to Christians who practice homosexuality or change their gender?

> *If the Spirit of God who raised Jesus from the dead dwells in you, then He who raised Jesus shall also give life to your earthly bodies through His Spirit, which is implanted in you. So then, brethren, you are debtors, but not debtors to the flesh, for if you live according to the flesh (various sinful desires), you will continue to experience spiritual death. However, if you live according to the Spirit, then you will find that because of the Spirit's presence, you are putting to death the deeds of the flesh. And in so doing you will experience the spiritual life God always intended for you to have. Therefore as many of you who are being led by the Spirit, you are called God's sons, daughters, and children. Romans 8:11-14 [RBK]*

Since homosexuality and gender change are sins according to the passages listed in Chapter 1, how is it possible for some Christians to claim these acts are okay? Disappointingly, many call themselves Christians who are simply not saved, yet, they think they are, for many different reasons. Some respect the life and ministry of Jesus but only think of Him as a great teacher or man, perhaps even the greatest ever. But, for the most part, they do not consider Him God, and, if they do, He is not the only God or path to salvation or heaven.

According to the Bible, if anyone or any church holds to this belief of Christ, they are likely "cultural Christians," but not genuine followers of Christ, even if they involve themselves in various charitable ministries or loving pursuits or go through the motions of weekly Christian worship.

> *Yet for us, there is but one God, the Father, from whom are all things and we exist for Him; and one Lord, Jesus Christ, by whom are all things, and we exist through Him. I Corinthians 8:6*

Jesus said, "I am the way, and the truth, and the life; no one comes to the Father but through Me." John 14:6

Therefore they said to Him, "What shall we do, so that we may work the works of God?" Jesus answered and said to them, "This is the work of God that you believe in Me whom He has sent." John 6:28-29

Everyone who hears these words of Mine and does not act on them will be like a foolish man who built his house on the sand. The rain fell, and the floods came, and the winds blew and slammed against that house, and it fell, and great was its fall. Matthew 7:26-27

Christians are those who begin their lives with repentance of all sins, none excluded, and faith in Christ. Nothing more is needed to be a Christian and nothing less. This new life begins to grow and develop proportionately to our obedience to God's written Word in all aspects, including its teaching on issues like homosexuality and gender change.

In our growth, God also gives Christians the Holy Spirit to help conquer old sins and patterns of wrongdoing. Salvation is never lost in this process, but what is gained is a new strengthening from the Spirit to do what is right, as well as His constant forgiveness and grace when we don't. *(John 14:16-17; 26; I Thessalonians 1:5; John 10:28; Hebrews 13:5; Matthew 28:20)*

The Spirit primarily uses the Scripture, the counsel of other Bible-believing Christians, and an inner sense of His presence to help us live according to God's will. When we feel troubled, anxious, or even guilty about sins like homosexuality or gender change, it is good because it shows the Spirit is at work in our lives. The quick solution is to ask for His immediate forgiveness, let Him be the Lord of us again, and walk in the Spirit as we go ahead with our lives.

For Christians who refuse to abide by the Spirit's work, they will struggle greatly, for part of the Spirit's ministry in us is to do battle with our *flesh* when we give into it. Some of the things we may experience in our struggles include increased depression, guilt, loss of vision, sickness, and even death. Remember though, in the midst of all of these possible consequences, God's love never wavers nor does He ever bring back any guilt that was taken care of at the cross. But He will, through the Spirit, do whatever is necessary to get us to abandon the *flesh* and return to walking in the Spirit which is the only thing that can bring peace to our lives.

The following Scriptures describe the inner struggle the Spirit allows or puts into our hearts as Christians when we sin. One comes from David, and the others are from Paul.

> *When I kept silent about my sin, my body wasted away through my groaning all day long. For day and night, Your hand was heavy upon me; my vitality was drained away as with the fever heat of summer. I acknowledged my sin to You, and my iniquity I did not hide; I said, I will confess my transgressions to the Lord, and You forgave the guilt of my sin. Psalm 32:3-5*

> *If you are living according to the flesh, you must die; but if by the Spirit you are putting to death the deeds of the body, you will live. Romans 8:13*

> *For I know that nothing good dwells in me, that is, in my flesh; for the willing is present in me, but the doing of the good is not. For the good that I want, I do not do, but I practice the very evil that I do not want. I find then the principle that evil is present in me, and the one who wants to do good. But I also see a different law in the members of my body, waging war against the law of my mind and making me a prisoner of the law of sin which is in my members. Wretched man that I am! Who will set me free from the body of this death?...There is therefore now no condemnation for those who are in Christ Jesus Romans 7:18-19, 21, 23-24, Romans 8:1*

Last Thought

How should Christians work with other Christians who claim to be homosexual, or have changed their gender? Although reprimands, rejections, and various reproofs are not easy to receive, they are appropriate and necessary for Christians to give to each other when these and other sins are committed. The Scriptures tell Christians to hold one another accountable when sins are committed. This kind of judging is okay, for it is not determining whether a person is going to heaven or not. Jesus alone is in charge of that.

Disciplining one another for regressing to old sins, or committing new ones is right to do, as long as it is done with prayer, love, and within the guidelines of the Bible. Failure to do so harms not only those who are sinning but the entire church which can be influenced by these wayward Christians.

The following Scriptures validate this kind of corrective-judging, one by James, one by Paul, and the last by Luke.

> *My brethren, if any among you strays from the truth and one turns him back, let him know that he who turns a sinner from the error of his way will save his soul from death and will cover a multitude of sins. James 5:19-20*

> *Now we command you, brethren, in the name of our Lord Jesus Christ that you keep away from every brother who leads an unruly life and not according to the tradition which you received from us. II Thessalonians 3:6*

> *Be on your guard! If your brother sins, rebuke him; and if he repents, forgive him. And if he sins against you seven times a day, and returns to you seven times, saying, "I repent, forgive him." Luke 17:3-4*

What do we do with Christians who say, "I am a believer and a homosexual; I feel comfortable about this and have no conflict or inner struggle from within with God?" What do you do with a Christian who has changed their gender and says the same thing? The absence of an inner struggle with sins like homosexuality or transgender change, strongly indicates the Spirit may not be residing within these proclaiming Christians, because the Spirit always goes to war within the heart of every Christian when the *flesh* is allowed to surface, live, and take control again. This whole inward battle is supported in Galatians five, which also lists many of the *fleshly* sins Christians encounter. Homosexuality, cross-dressing [forerunner to gender change], and being effeminate [forerunner to gender change] is not mentioned in this list but are in other Scriptures describing sins of the *flesh*. (See I Timothy 1:8-11, I Corinthians 6:9-11, and Deuteronomy 22:5 in Chapter 1).

> *[16] But I say, walk by the Spirit, and you will not carry out the desire of the flesh. [17] For the flesh sets its desire against the Spirit, and*

the Spirit against the flesh; for these are in opposition to one another, so that you may not do the things that you please. [19] Now the deeds of the flesh are evident, which are: immorality, impurity, sensuality, [20] idolatry, sorcery, enmities, strife, jealousy, outbursts of anger, disputes, dissensions, factions, [21] envying, drunkenness, carousing, and things like these, of which I forewarn you, just as I have forewarned you, that those who practice such things will not inherit the kingdom of God. Galatians 5:16-17, 19-21

When Christians enter into sin and let the *flesh* reign once again, this also grieves the Spirit greatly. Since He lives in us, and always will, we should begin to feel His grief and eventually enter into it with Him. Hopefully, this grief will be another reason to abandon our *flesh*. If a Christian claims to be homosexual, and there is no grief within, the absence of the Spirit is once again very possible. And if there is no Spirit, then there can be no genuine salvation experience.

[30] Do not grieve the Holy Spirit of God, by whom you were sealed for the day of redemption. [31] Let all bitterness and wrath and anger and clamor and slander be put away from you, along with all malice. [32] Be kind to one another, tender-hearted, forgiving each other, just as God in Christ also has forgiven you. Ephesians 4:30-32

In ministering to those who claim to be Christians but have fallen into homosexuality or changed their gender, it is best to treat them as non-Christians because likely that is what they are. In doing this, we don't need to reject them, but love them the best we can, spend as much time with them as possible, help them when help is needed, pray for their salvation, and present the Gospel to them as if they had never heard it before. After all of this, we should repeat the process again and patiently wait for them to believe, repent, or change. During our waiting we should never accept their homosexuality or gender change as right, for that would be contrary to what the Spirit is doing within them.

Should they ask us how we feel about them being gay, we should tell them the truth about it as lovingly as we can and be sure to point to the Scriptures when we do this. If they repeatedly reject what we say, then it may be time to move on to others who need discipling or Jesus' message of salvation. There are too many in this world who need Him, and we don't want to neglect them for the sake of those who continually hang onto their own sins and refuse to put their faith in God.

Scripture References

John 14:16-17, 26 *¹⁶I will ask the Father, and He will give you another Helper, that He may be with you forever; ¹⁷that is the Spirit of truth, whom the world cannot receive, because it does not see Him or know Him, but you know Him because He abides with you and will be in you. ²⁶But the Helper, the Holy Spirit, whom the Father will send in My name, He will teach you all things, and bring to your remembrance all that I said to you.*

I Thessalonians 1:5 *For our gospel did not come to you in word only, but also in power and in the Holy Spirit and with full conviction; just as you know what kind of men we proved to be among you for your sake.*

John 10:28 *I give them eternal life, and they will never perish, and no one will snatch them out of my hand.*

Hebrews 13:5 & Matthew 28:20 *I will never desert you nor forsake you… for I am with you always, even to the end of the age.*

This chapter is based on 44 verses in 21 passages of Scripture

Chapter 9

Judging the LGBT Community

Is it right to judge members of the LGBT Community for their practices?

> *Speak the truth in love... Better is open rebuke than love concealed. Faithful are the wounds of a friend. Ephesians 4:15 & Proverbs 27:5-6*

I don't know how many times I've heard over the years the words, "You shouldn't judge others," or "You're not supposed to judge if you are a Christian," or "I thought only God was to judge." These comments have a degree of truth based on what Jesus said in the course of His ministry, but they don't tell the whole truth.

There are two major kinds of judging in God's Word, one that has to do with judging another's salvation and the other with holding each other accountable to God's laws, commands, and principles. This latter kind of judging involves encouraging, admonishing, correcting, and reprimanding those who disobey or ignore God's teaching and warning against various wrongdoings and practices.

Here are a few of the many passages that cover judging. They are intertwined with one another to show that to judge (correct) and not to judge are appropriate for Christians to do, depending upon the circumstances.

> *My brethren, if any among you strays from the truth and one turns him back, let him know that he who turns a sinner from the error of his way will save his soul from death and will cover a multitude of sins. James 5:19-20*

> *Do not speak against one another, brethren. He, who speaks against a brother or judges his brother, speaks against the law and judges the law; but if you judge the law, you are not a doer of the law but a judge of it. There are only one Lawgiver and Judge, the One who is able to save and to destroy; but who are you who judge your neighbor? James 4:11-12*

Do you not know that Christians (saints) will judge the world? If the world is judged by you, are you not competent to constitute the smallest law courts? Do you not know that we will judge angels? How much more matters of this life? I Corinthians 6:2-3

Do not judge so that you will not be judged. For in the way you judge, you will be judged; and by your standard of measure, it will be measured to you. Matthew 7:1-2

Jesus said, "Be on your guard! If your brother sins, rebuke him; and if he repents, forgive him." Luke 17:3

I solemnly charge you in the presence of God and of Christ Jesus, who is to judge the living and the dead, and by His appearing and His kingdom: preach the word; be ready in season and out of season; reprove, rebuke, exhort, with great patience and instruction. For the time will come when they will not endure sound doctrine; but wanting to have their ears tickled, they will accumulate for themselves teachers in accordance to their own desires and will turn away their ears from the truth and will turn aside to myths. II Timothy 4:1-4

The mouth of the righteous speaks wisdom, and their tongues talk of judgment. Psalm 37:30 (King James Version)

    What set of circumstances would authorize Christians to judge and correct others? The answer lies in whether an action can be identified as sin according to Scripture. If something is done that is sinful and harmful to others, then the one doing it may need to be judged and corrected. As we judge in this respect, which I like to call a correction, we should rebuke on one end, but encourage on the other. We should lace what we say and do with as much love as can be mustered.

    Due to our faith in Christ, God has chosen us as ambassadors to represent His truth. Part of being a good ambassador is to openly expose the presence, reality, and destructiveness of sin. Without such exposure, wrongdoings can spread and rule the entire world. We have seen this over and over again as demonstrated when evil and sinful men have taken control of different cultures and nations.

I am an ambassador in chains; that in proclaiming it I may speak boldly, as I ought to speak. Ephesians 6:20

To better understand how Christians are to judge correctly and hold others accountable for their sins, there are four paths to follow that I call The Gavel Path, The Logjam Path, The Path of Missing-the-Mark, and The Path of Rescue.

The Gavel Path

In an American courtroom, there are some key participants; the most important is the judge who controls the proceedings. The judge uses a gavel to maintain control of the courtroom, and, if needed, end a particular discussion on an issue. When this wooden-like hammer is pounded on the judge's desk, everyone must stop what they are saying or doing. They do this because of the judge's authority. Hence, over time, the gavel has become a symbol of the judge's power to make decisions, especially the one that ends a case.

This illustration is similar to Jesus who was given the responsibility to judge who is worthy to enter into the kingdom of God and who isn't. This doesn't mean God the Father and the Spirit are not also involved in judging the actions of those they created, yet Jesus was chosen to do their bidding on the final Day of Judgment when He returns a second and last time. *(I Thessalonians 4:16-17; John 5:22; John 8:16)* When Jesus said to the disciples in the Sermon on the Mount, "Do not judge," He was telling them, and all Christians, not to usurp His role as judge of another's salvation.

There are a few reasons why Jesus does not want us to judge in this respect. The foremost is that we are not equipped to know the heart of another, as He does, no matter how spiritual or knowledgeable we think we are. Unlike us, Jesus can look beyond everyone's words and actions and see who they are regarding a saving faith. *(I Corinthians 4:5; Luke 16:15)*

Therefore, when we are tempted to say to those in the LGBT Community that they are not going to enter the kingdom of heaven because of what they are doing, don't! This is not our role! We should say, instead, that God through His Scripture says that you need to believe and repent of all of your sins, including your gay practices, to enter the kingdom. The key is to leave them with His Scripture for their spiritual destiny, even though our words or opinions may sound exactly like what the Scriptures teach. This may seem like a slight point, but it is not, because by doing this, it removes us from being their judge for salvation.

    Here are a few of many passages to share with those who have elected to be gay, or who have changed their gender, or committed any other sin as far as that is concerned. All of these verses speak of the salvation needed first before any real and lasting change can take place.

> *Jesus said, "I tell you that unless you repent, you will perish." Luke 13:3*
>
> *Jesus said, "I am the way, the truth, and the life; no one comes to the Father but through Me." John 14:6*
>
> *If you confess with your mouth Jesus as Lord and believe in your heart that God raised Him from the dead, you will be saved; for with the heart a person believes, resulting in righteousness, and with the mouth, he confesses, resulting in salvation. For the Scripture says, "Whoever believes in Him will not be disappointed." Romans 10:9-11*
>
> *Whoever believes will in Him have eternal life. For God so loved the world that He gave His only begotten Son, that whoever believes in Him shall not perish, but have eternal life. John 3:15-16*

The Logjam Path

    Once, when I was dieting, I ran across a gal who was extremely overweight. I could not help but eavesdrop on a conversation she was having with a friend as she advised what to eat to keep trim and healthy. Later, I saw her munching on a candy bar in one hand and devouring an ice cream cone in the other. Needless to say, I threw out any advice I heard her say about keeping trim. In my estimation, she was a hypocrite, saying one thing but doing the opposite. Comparably, this is what I believe Jesus was saying about many of the religious leaders of His day, who ruthlessly judged the spiritual lives of others, yet lived the opposite. Jesus made this point right after He warned against judging another's salvation in the Sermon on the Mount using a "log in the eye" illustration. He said, *"Why do you look at the speck in your brother's eye, but do not notice the log in your own eye? How can you say to your brother, let me take the speck out of your eye, and behold, a log is in your own eye? You hypocrite, first take the log out of your own eye, and then you will see clearly to take the speck out of your brother's eye." Matthew 7:3-5*

We had better get our own lives together before speaking into the lives of others. When addressing those in the LGBT Community, we can't be involved in other immoral acts of our own. Just because our transgressions are done from a heterosexual root doesn't make them less wrong. This doesn't mean we have to be perfect before confronting others about their sins, but we need to make every effort to be right with the Lord in our own lives. Often, this means nothing more than recognizing our sins and then asking Jesus to forgive us.

If perfection is the necessary criteria before confronting others, then nothing would ever be said or done. If nothing is ever said or done about sin, then there would be no restraint to the horrific things we could continue to do to others and ourselves. Two World Wars and atrocities attached to them are proof of sin that was initially ignored, discounted, or unchallenged.

Therefore, we are to get rid of the logjam of sin in our own lives first, so that we can effectively help those committing homosexually related sins. If we don't, then the judging and correcting God wants us to do will fall on deaf ears.

The Path of Missing-the-Mark

When I was young, I took up archery for a season. It was a unique activity and different than other sports like basketball and football that had previously drawn my interest. The goal of archery was to shoot an arrow and hit the middle of the target called the bullseye. It was easier to do this from close range, but harder when I moved farther away. I was not very good at archery; my arrows often missed the bullseye. Maybe if I had been coached by someone who knew what they were doing, I would have done better. But that was not the case, so I eventually lost interest and gave my bow and arrows to a friend.

In a way, missing the bullseye in my experience is like the misjudging of which Paul was critical. In the passages quoted within this chapter *(Ephesians 4:15, I Corinthians 6:2-3, II Timothy 4:1-4, I Corinthians 6:9-10)*, Paul indicates there is accountability we incur when we judge and correct others. Our intent should be to rescue them from their transgressions. A key to doing this well is first to establish if something is actually a sin. If it is, then the Bible will identify it as such in several different places, as it has with homosexuality. If it is established as sin, then it needs to be confronted, exhorted, and corrected.

As avid as Paul was in encouraging fellow believers to confront others about sin, he was just as fervent in scolding them when they went too far and judged practices that were not specifically condemned in God's Word. To him, this type of judging was deeply flawed and missed the bullseye when trying to help others.

When we read in Paul's letters of his disapproval of judging, it never involves a reversal of a clearly stated sin. There were rules and certain practices in the Old Testament that required obedience, but not so when the New Testament era began. Some practices that were questioned in Paul's day involved eating, drinking, and worshipping. None of these Old Testament practices were inherently evil, but rather customs that were decided upon by each believer and the Lord, according to their particular circumstance or culture. Homosexuality, effeminacy, cross-dressing, and eventual gender change, on the other hand, were identified as sinful in every era in the Bible and needed to be judged, rebuked, and stopped.

The following passage in Romans is an example of Paul's teaching about judging on issues that can go many ways with God and His will. Colossians 2:16-23 and I Corinthians 10:25-32 are two other passages that teach the same.

> *One person has faith that he may eat all things, but he who is weak eats vegetables only. The one who eats is not to regard with contempt the one who does not eat, and the one who does not eat is not to judge the one who eats, for God has accepted him. Who are you to judge the servant of another? One person regards one day above another; another regards every day alike. Each person must be fully convinced in his own mind. He, who observes the day, observes it for the Lord, and he who eats, does so for the Lord, for he gives thanks to God; and he who eats not, for the Lord he does*

not eat, and gives thanks to God. But you, why do you judge your brother? Therefore, let us not judge one another anymore, but rather determine this --not to put an obstacle or a stumbling block in a brother's way. It is good not to eat meat or to drink wine, or to do anything by which your brother stumbles. The faith which you have should be your own conviction before God. Happy is he who does not condemn himself in what he approves. But he who doubts is condemned if he eats because his eating is not from faith, and whatever is not from faith is a sin. Romans 14:2-3, 6, 10, 13, 21-23

The Path of Rescue

When my son was in high school, he worked as a lifeguard at Lake Almanor in California. During one particular summer, he saved a couple of children from drowning. On one occasion, a young boy got caught underneath the diving dock, but Brodie saw the situation and immediately swam out and pulled him free. The boy's mother, who stood on the shore, was very appreciative, as you can imagine. The main reason Brodie was able to do what he did that day was that he had been trained. My son is now on a different life-saving undertaking as a missionary to the Republic of Georgia near Ukraine.

Similarly, we are like Brodie when we jump in and try to save others who are drowning in their transgressions. Part of our effort to rescue them involves telling them what their wrongs are according to God's Word. Thus, for those tied to the LGBT practices, it means telling them that what they are doing is sinful. Not to reprove them is like letting them drown in their iniquities and immoralities.

Jesus is the model for rescuing others from sin. He not only loved, but also taught, and gave others grace and forgiveness; He also brought their sins to their attention. Jesus was often compassionate when pointing out wrongdoings but was never quiet or remiss in exposing them. The case of the woman caught in adultery is an example because, at the end of saving her from being stoned for her offense, Jesus turned and said, "Now, go and sin no more." In other words, "You were wrong in what you were doing, but I have rescued and forgiven you, now quit sinning." *(John 8:5, 7, 9-11)*

At other times, Jesus was not quite as compassionate, but rather confrontational in His judging, as was the case with many of the religious leaders of His day. Sometimes He even called them hypocrites because they refused to give mercy, justice, and forgiveness to the people they were called to lead and serve. *(Matthew 23:23, 28)*

When applying Christ's example, employ either a compassionate or confrontational approach according to the person with whom you are dealing. For those who are clearly saved and a part of the church, a more confrontational approach may be needed for they should know better. However, for those outside of the church who need salvation more than anything else, a gentler approach may be appropriate. A gentler approach may also be best for some inside of the church depending upon their sin and circumstance. The following Scripture demonstrates this two-pronged approach.

Confrontational Approach (geared toward noncompliant Christians)

It is actually reported that there is immorality among you, and immorality of such a kind as does not exist even among the Gentiles, that someone has his father's wife. You have become arrogant and have not mourned instead so that the one who had done this deed would be removed from your midst. For I, on my part, though absent in body but present in spirit, have already judged him who has so committed this, as though I were present. In the name of our Lord Jesus, when you are assembled, and I with you in spirit, with the power of our Lord Jesus, I have decided to deliver such a one to Satan for the destruction of his flesh, so that his spirit may be saved in the day of the Lord Jesus. Your boasting is not good. Do you not know that a little leaven leavens the whole lump of dough? Clean out the old leaven so that you may be a new lump, just as you are in fact unleavened. For Christ, our Passover also has been sacrificed. Therefore, let us celebrate the feast, not with old leaven, nor with the leaven of malice and wickedness, but with the unleavened bread of sincerity and truth. I wrote you in my letter not to associate with immoral people; I did not at all mean with the immoral people of this world, or with the covetous and swindlers, or with idolaters, for then you would have to go out of the world. But actually, I wrote to you not to associate with any so-

called brother if he is an immoral person, or covetous, or an idolater, or a reviler, or a drunkard, or a swindler—not even to eat with such a one. For what have I to do with judging outsiders? Do you not judge those who are within the church? But God judges those on the outside; therefore, remove the wicked man from among yourselves. I Corinthians 5:1-13

Gentle Approach (geared toward non-Christians and Christians)

The Lord's bond-servant must not be quarrelsome, but be kind to all, able to teach, patient when wronged, with gentleness correcting those who are in opposition, if perhaps God may grant them repentance leading to the knowledge of the truth, and they may come to their senses and escape from the snare of the devil, having been held captive by him to do his will. II Timothy 2:24-26,

Brethren, even if a man is caught in any trespass, you who are spiritual, restore such a one in a spirit of gentleness; looking to yourself, lest you too be tempted. Gal 6:1

"And if your brother sins go and reprove him in private; if he listens to you, you have won your brother." Matt 18:15

Last Thoughts

Is it right for Christians to judge and correct others who are caught up in the LGBT Community? The overall answer is "yes," except concerning judging their salvation or entry into God's kingdom. That is for Jesus to do, and only Him. Outside of this, it's our responsibility as God's ambassadors to share His truth with them about everything, including their sins.

Scripture References

I Thessalonians 4:16-17 *[16]For the Lord Himself will descend from heaven with a shout, with the voice of the archangel and with the trumpet of God, and the dead in Christ will rise first. [17]Then we who are alive and remain will be caught up together with them in the clouds to meet the Lord in the air, and so we shall always be with the Lord.*

John 5:22 *Not even the Father judges anyone, but He has given all judgment to the Son.*

John 8:16 *But even if I do judge, My judgment is true; for I am not alone in it, but I and the Father who sent Me.*

I Corinthians 4:5 *Therefore do not go on passing judgment before the time but wait until the Lord comes who will both bring to light the things hidden in the darkness and disclose the motives of men's hearts.*

Luke 16:15 *And He said to them, you are those who justify yourselves in the sight of men, but God knows your hearts; for that which is highly esteemed among men is detestable in the sight of God.*

John 8:5, 7, 9-11 *[5]Now in the Law Moses commanded us to stone such women; what then do You say? [7]But when they persisted in asking Him, He straightened up, and said to them, he who is without sin among you let him be the first to throw a stone at her. [9]When they heard it, they began to go out one by one, beginning with the older ones, and He was left alone with the woman. [10]Straightening up, Jesus said to her, "Woman, where are they? Did no one condemn you? [11]She said, "No one, Lord. And Jesus said, "I do not condemn you, either. Go and from now on sin no more."*

Matthew 23:23, 28 *[23]Woe to you, scribes and Pharisees, hypocrites! For you tithe mint and dill and cummin and have neglected the weightier provisions of the law: justice and mercy and faithfulness; but these are the things you should have done without neglecting the others. [28]So you, too, outwardly appear righteous to men, but inwardly you are full of hypocrisy and lawlessness.*

This chapter is based on 79 verses in 28 passages of Scripture

Chapter 10

Churches that Validate the LGBT Agenda

How should Christians respond to churches that validate the LGBT agenda?

> *There will also be false teachers among you, who will secretly introduce destructive heresies, and many will follow their sensuality, and because of them the way of the truth will be much maligned. II Peter 2:1-2*

There are a growing number of churches today that validate the gay lifestyle, and even encourage those who want to alter their gender. They believe this is compassionate and shows "Christian" love to the fullest; criticizing churches that don't, even though the Scriptures clearly condemn these practices as shown in Chapter 1.

There are five possible reasons why many of these churches take this stand. The first is they see themselves as having Jesus-type compassion for all people, especially those in the LGBT community. Therefore, their worship services, Sunday schools, and leadership ranks are very inclusive of gays and those who have changed their gender. They reason, if Jesus accepted the rejected people of His day, like Mary Magdalene and the woman caught in adultery, then why shouldn't Christians do the same for those in the LGBT communities today? *(Luke 8:1-2)* To adopt this view, though, the leaders, pastors, priests, and congregants of these churches ignore or dismiss the Scriptures that deal with the prohibition of homosexuality and its related groups.

Churches that ignore or deny God's written Word for the sake of a particular belief or feeling are usually called liberal churches. In effect, they give more weight to their own expertise, opinions, and preferences on issues like homosexuality, than what the Scriptures teach. The bottom line is they don't trust the Bible to be the inspired and infallible Word of God, even though this is what the Scriptures claim. This leaves each of us with a decision to make to believe what Scriptures teach or to put our trust in what the liberal leaders of these churches say.

> *All Scripture is inspired by God and profitable for teaching, for reproof, for correction, for training in righteousness; so that the*

man of God may be adequate, equipped for every good work. II Timothy 3:16-17

A second reason liberal-minded churches embrace homosexuality is they typically apply the parts of God's grace to which they agree. They love God's compassion, mercy, and acceptance, but play down His forgiveness in their theology. They do this because forgiveness indicates something is wrong or needs to be changed. By and large, committed homosexuals embrace this liberal theology of "I'm OK, and I'm living right" because they see no need to be forgiven for what they are doing. When they choose a church, they not only want to "come as they are" but stay as they are, heart, head, lifestyle and all.

But this is not an accurate or complete view of grace according to the Scriptures, because forgiveness was the central part of what Jesus did on the cross when He died for our sins. All we need to do is repent and believe to receive His forgiveness. This is a message liberal churches stay away from when dealing with the LGBT community.

A third reason these churches welcome those committed to the LGBT agenda is that they are afraid to do otherwise for culture dictates their theology and practice. Like it or not, they do what society tells them to do. For the moment, the media and a vocal portion of our American society are telling churches to get rid of their old theology rules and cautions. If they don't, then they will be accused of being intolerant, unloving, and even racist. Regrettably, these liberal churches have yielded to and complied with contemporary society's demands and opinions.

A fourth reason some congregations accept homosexuality is that their leaders and pastors are homosexual or transgender people themselves. It should be of no surprise, then, these leaders and pastors have a lot to say about what their people hold to and believe. The result is the lifestyles and practices of these church leaders supplant what God's Word teaches about homosexuality.

The final reason churches accept the LGBT agenda against which the Bible warns or teaches is that their leaders are simply not genuine believers. If this is true, and only God knows for sure, then these leaders never actually repented of their sins, nor did they make Jesus the Lord of their lives. Hence, they advocate beliefs that run counter to the Scriptures.

Jesus experienced leaders like these during His ministry, who held religious positions, quoted Scripture, and seemingly did good works, but never completely gave their hearts or minds to God. When Jesus encountered them, He was very frank, telling them they were filled with iniquity and would not inherit God's kingdom.

> *Not everyone that says unto me, "Lord, Lord," will enter into the kingdom of heaven; but he that does the will of my Father who is in heaven. Many will say to me on that day, "Lord, Lord, did we not prophesy by your name, and in your name cast out demons, and in your name perform many miracles?" And then will I declare to them, "I never knew you: depart from me, you who practice lawlessness." Matthew 7:21-23*

Churches that do not endorse or believe in the Scriptures run the risk of becoming apostate churches, against which the Scripture strongly warns. *(II Thessalonians 2:3; Jeremiah 14:7)* Apostate churches are those that do not see Christ as the only way to salvation, or the Bible as God's central expression of His will or Word but substitute something else instead.

Individuals who have sunk into apostasy have fallen away from their faith; in other words, have de-converted from their original belief in Christ and Christianity. Regrettably, there are churches and individual Christians today who have already gone down the apostasy path. Were they Christian in the first place? I don't know, that is up to Christ to judge. Will they ever return to their faith? The Scripture seems to indicate they won't, for they are set on an unalterable course, having seen true faith and walked away from it, much like Judas.

> *For in the case of those who have once been enlightened and have tasted of the heavenly gift and have been made partakers of the Holy Spirit, and have tasted the good word of God and the powers of the age to come, and then have fallen away, it is impossible to renew them again to repentance, since they again crucify to themselves the Son of God and put Him to open shame. Hebrews 6:4-6*

The point is not to go down a path that leads to apostasy, whether as a church or an individual. To avoid this, make the Scripture the entire basis for what we believe on all issues, including what it says about practices like homosexuality. If we don't then we are vulnerable to compromise on the next issue, and then the next, and the next, until we have nothing left in the Bible in which to believe. This is what theological liberalism did in the 19th century.

If we are in churches that follow God's Word in respect to the LGBT agenda, then be thankful, for we are following what God wants us to believe. However, as we look at other churches who don't believe as we do, then begin to pray for them in earnest. Don't just sit around and criticize or belittle them for being liberal or even apostate; that will not help them discover the truth. Although we don't agree with their views, still be kind and loving toward them. Perhaps by doing so, we can earn the opportunity to share with individuals in those churches God's truth in Scripture.

Will they listen or reverse their views because of our love or what we share? They may not, but we should always seek to proclaim the truth faithfully. The Bible seems to indicate that most of these churches won't change their minds or their ways. *(II Timothy 4:3-4)* Nevertheless, keep praying and sharing the truth, perhaps a few of their members might be impacted and swayed.

On another note, if we continue in a church that supports the LGBT agenda and we want to do something about it, there are three possible avenues to pursue:

The first avenue is to share with the leaders and members of these churches what the Scriptures teach about homosexuality. It could be they have never read or delved into the passages that condemn homosexuality and gender change. In other words, it may be new news to them. If we are successful and they decide to change their stance, then we have done a very good thing for God. In truth, helping them reverse such a belief is perhaps one of the reasons God put each of us in our churches in the first place.

The second avenue is to be less assertive and take a behind-the-scenes sort of approach. This involves quietly praying for the leadership in our church. In our petitions to God, pray these leaders will align themselves with what Scripture teaches on these condemned practices. If they don't change after a significant time of prayer, then ask God to replace them with other leaders who will completely trust God's inspired Word in what they teach. If this doesn't work either, then the third and last avenue is to leave this church for another that follows and abides by the Scripture.

Last Thoughts

Over the last several years, I've visited several churches that have embraced the LGBT agenda. One of the reasons was I wanted to see how they reached out and ministered to gays and transgender people. My most significant observation was how inclusive these churches were with all groups of people including men with men, women with women, men posing as women, or women posing as men. All were okay in their sight and very much welcomed.

In a way, these churches reminded me somewhat of churches I attended in the '60s that reached out to the uninhibited youth of that era who wore long hair, went barefoot, dressed like hippies, lived in communes, practiced open sex, protested the Vietnam war, and did drugs of all kinds. As a result of their welcoming attitudes, multitudes of young people heard the Gospel for the first time, received Christ as Lord and Savior, and began to abandon behaviors and habits contrary to God's will. It was the verses of the Bible that helped them the most in making changes in their behaviors and lifestyles, along with the Holy Spirit, of course. For some, the long hair and bare feet remained, but the open sex and drugs quickly went by the wayside because of what was taught from the Bible. Unfortunately, many Bible-believing churches I attended during that time did not do as well in reaching these young people and missed a great opportunity!

Although there is a similarity between welcoming churches of the '60s and the liberal churches of today, there is also a huge difference. The great difference is not in the welcoming, acceptance, or even the unconditional love conveyed and displayed, but in what is hoped. The churches of the '60s hoped the young people of their day would eventually find Christ and ask Him into their hearts for salvation. After which they anticipated these young peoples' lives would change over time due to an indwelling Spirit, discipleship, and teaching from the Scriptures. With this hope in mind, they were willing and eager to accept the young people as they were when they showed up, no matter what they had done.

To the contrary, the hope of liberal churches today that validate the LGBT agenda relies on a revised view of God's grace that allows everyone to do and be whatever they want, even if it runs counter to the teachings of the Bible. Therefore, gays go about being unrepentant in these churches, and transgender people do the same. The outcome is disastrous, for this leads to no real spiritual relief, or salvation because what is missing is the forgiveness of their sins.

If there is anything to be learned from this with the Bible-believing churches of today, all need to be very welcoming toward LGBT members, but then pursue teaching them God's Word about what they are doing in a very loving and patient way just as the churches of the '60s did with the young people of their generation.

Scripture References

Luke 8:1-2 *¹Soon afterward, He began going around from one city and village to another, proclaiming and preaching the kingdom of God. The twelve were with Him, ²and also some women who had been healed of evil spirits and sicknesses: Mary who was called Magdalene, from whom seven demons had gone out.*

II Thessalonian 2:3 *Let no one in any way deceive you, for it will not come unless the apostasy comes first, and the man of lawlessness is revealed, the son of destruction.*

Jeremiah 14:7 *Although our iniquities testify against us, O Lord, act for Your name's sake! Truly our apostasies have been many, for we have sinned against You.*

II Timothy 4:3-4 *³For the time will come when they will not endure sound doctrine, but wanting to have their ears tickled, they will accumulate for themselves teachers in accordance to their own desires. ⁴They will turn away their ears from the truth and will turn aside to myths.*

This chapter is based on 17 verses in 8 passages of Scripture

Chapter 11

Government Leaders, Justices, and Educators that Legislate for the LGBT Agenda

What actions should Christians take with politicians, government leaders, justices, and educators who continually support and legislate for the LGBT agenda?

Blessed is the nation whose God is the Lord. Psalm 33:12

Benjamin Franklin, along with the majority of other founding leaders of this nation, understood that if America was to succeed, then God needed to be recognized, honored, and valued. For Franklin to say this was significant because he wrestled throughout his life with his Christian beliefs.

> *"I've lived, sir, a long time, and the longer I live, the more I am convinced that God governs in the affairs of men. And if a sparrow cannot fall to the ground without the Lord's notice, how is it possible that a nation can rise without His aid? For without the Lord building the house, all who labor, do so in vain."* [1] *Benjamin Franklin*

In the early years of America, dependence on God and His Word as recorded in the Bible was one of the foundation pieces that helped our leaders make many turning-point decisions. Abolition of slavery was just one of those decisions which were strongly rooted in Scripture.

> *There is neither Jew nor Greek; there is neither slave nor free, there is no male and female, for you are all one in Christ Jesus. Galatians 3:28*

As evidenced by their own words, many of these early founders and leaders did not hesitate to openly declare their respect for God, faith in Christ, knowledge of sin, and love for the principles of the Scripture when making decisions, rulings, and judgments as shown in these comments.

"O blessed Father, let thy Son's blood wash me from all impurities, and cleanse me from the stains of sin that are upon me. Give me the grace to lay hold of Your merits; that they may be my conciliation and atonement. May I know my sins are forgiven, by Your Son's death and resurrection?" [2] *President George Washington*

"The Declaration of Independence laid the cornerstone of human government upon the first precepts of Christianity, for I have examined all religions, and the result is that the Bible is the best book in the world." [3] *President John Adams*

"We have been the recipients of the choicest bounties of heaven. We have been preserved these many years in peace and prosperity. We have grown in numbers, wealth and power as no other nation has ever grown. But we have forgotten God. It behooves us then to humble ourselves before the offended powers, to confess our national sins and to pray for clemency and forgiveness." [4] *President Abraham Lincoln*

"Let the children who are sent to those schools be taught to read, write, and above all let both sexes be carefully instructed in the principles and obligations of the Christian religion. This is the most essential part of education." [5] *Benjamin Rush (Signer of Declaration of Independence)*

"Education is useless without the Bible." [6] *Daniel Webster*

"Cursed be all learning that is contrary to the cross of Christ." [7] *President James Madison*

Many leaders in subsequent generations followed in these founders' footsteps making God and His Word an important part of their decisions. Examples of their dedication lie in the phrases they eventually put on our currency and in the pledge of allegiance, "In God, We Trust adopted in 1936," and "One Nation under God added in 1954."

In the 1960s, however, honoring God and the Bible sharply faded from the decisions made by many of America's government officials, politicians, judges, and educational leaders. As a result, the principles of Scripture, which were once respected by so many leaders of the past, became ignored, downplayed and even censored.

Amid this new era of American leadership, the Bible and its views have been suppressed on educational issues like school prayer, the presence of the Bible in a classroom, and creationism taught alongside evolution. Easter holidays have been dubbed as Spring Break, Christmas Vacation has become Winter Holiday, and the Ten Commandments, the cross of Jesus, and Christmas manger scenes have been banned from most campuses. Also, for the first time, homosexuality, same-sex marriage, and gender change of which the Bible strongly condemns have not only become acceptable with educational leaders but also a part of their constantly-changing curriculums. *(See Leviticus 20:13, Deuteronomy 22:5, I Timothy 1:8-11 and I Corinthians 6:9-11 in Chapter 1)*

Why have so many of our current leaders deserted the Scriptures and traditional Christian values when it comes to making decisions on our behalf? Regrettably, many are not like past leaders because they simply don't have the same faith in God. Without such a faith these leaders have let their sin natures (with which we were all born) flourish and affect their thinking and reasoning. They have thrown out God's Word when making decisions, unlike George Washington, Abraham Lincoln, and other past leaders. Unless today's leaders change and make Christ the Lord of their lives, then they will continue to corrupt us morally and spiritually until nothing is left of what we used to believe in or depend upon as a nation.

The following two passages of Scripture are great guides for our leaders should they consider reversing their course and begin trusting God. But I am afraid things would have to get pretty grim for us as a country before such a turnabout took place with our leaders. Knowing this, perhaps our prayers should change, and instead of praying for our nation's morality and spirituality, which are good prayers, perhaps we should pray that we go through some very difficult times as a nation so that our leaders would spiritually wake up and lead us as God would have them. Something to think about the next time we pray for our leaders and this nation.

If you confess with your mouth Jesus as Lord and believe in your heart that God raised Him from the dead, you will be saved; for with the heart a person believes, resulting in righteousness, and with the mouth, he confesses, resulting in salvation. Romans 10:9-10

I acknowledged my sin to You, oh Lord, and my iniquity I did not hide; and You forgave the guilt of my sin. Psalm 32:5

    If spiritual transformation does not take place with our leaders, then issues like homosexuality, gender change, and same-sex marriage will continue to win out in our culture. These leaders may openly acknowledge God, go to church, give public prayers, and even quote Scripture in their speeches but then turn around and support issues that are condemned in the Bible, like abortion, euthanasia, and homosexuality. What is surprising is that they seemingly do this without any inner conflict, which is possible evidence the Spirit of God does not actually reside within them. If they had the Spirit, which is given to all true believers, then that Spirit would be at war within their souls about what they are doing. Once again only Christ truly knows if they have the Spirit or not, but as followers of Him, we should be able to recognize "false" Christians who say one thing but do the opposite. The bottom line is we need more genuine Christians to enter the different ranks of leadership in our country; Christians who struggle within when they sin or go against God's Word on an issue.

    God has allowed the LGBT agenda to prevail in our court rulings and law-making for a few reasons. As history shows throughout the Bible, the Lord often does not immediately respond with judgment when a nation, or even a person, turn against Him or His Word on moral issues. Instead, He lets them experience, at least for a season, the negative consequences that come from making such determinations. Those consequences often include confusion about what is truly right or wrong, increased sexual immorality, an upsurge in crime, financial setbacks, gross conduct within the leadership, and a growing lack of respect amongst other nations.

    God may also allow the homosexual agenda to prevail in our latest government rulings because He wants Christians and churches to wake up and start playing the role they were always intended to play, which is to reach out and win over those consumed by these sins. Had Christians and churches taken on this ministry at the very beginning, then, perhaps, the conflicts we have today over these Biblically-condemned practices would not be so prevalent. But it's not too late to get on board with the Lord in ministering to these people. All we need do is start reaching them with the love of God on the one hand and the truth of Scriptures about their sin on the other.

In addition to sharing the saving message of Christ with gay or transgender people, we can also support genuine Christians who run for leadership positions. We do this by praying for these brave souls, voting and campaigning for them, and even financially supporting their efforts.

We might also petition and push for new laws to limit the terms and powers of leaders who run counter to God's Word in their decision making. By implementing new and revised laws, adversarial leaders might be removed from office before it is too late. A couple of ideas to carry this out are term limits for Federal judges and Supreme Court justices. Furthermore, these important positions should be voted on by the people, rather than appointed by the higher-ups in government. Many Americans have grown weary of the decisions made by our judiciary over the last few years, especially those that run counter to the feelings and desires of the majority. It is time for this to stop and change.

Last Thoughts

Though America seems to be making a shift toward accepting homosexuality as moral and normal, it is still not the majority opinion of most. At least as of 2018, it isn't. Acceptance of homosexuality, same-sex marriage, and transgender people are also not the majority opinion of most nations in the world. Eighty-three nations today outlaw homosexuality, making it a crime to practice. A similar number of other nations allow it, but not same-sex marriage. So as Christians we should not feel alone and isolated in our thinking when it comes to battling these practices and lifestyles in America.[8]

Where is America headed if we keep making rulings and laws that run counter to God's teachings? Before answering, there is still time to reverse the anti-Biblical rulings our country's leaders have been making. If we do this, then as a nation we could again become a great moral leader and influence on other nations. If we don't, the current decisions on homosexuality and other issues that run counter to the Scriptures could lead possibly to the collapse of America as a nation. In Biblical prophecy, the end times identify some great nations and, amazingly, America is not mentioned as one of them. Perhaps, it is because we crumble as a world power.

If America's collapse does come, and I pray it doesn't, then there are several ways God will allow this to happen. The first will be similar to the way He treated His own beloved Israel when that nation walked away from His teachings. The second is how He dealt with the mighty and morally corrupt Roman Empire.

God allowed other world powers to defeat and enslave Israel because of its desertion from His truth and laws. The people of Israel remained enslaved until they changed their hearts and started trusting God and His Word again. Sad to say for their sakes, it took many decades for them to come to this decision.

> *Thus, the Israelites became unclean in their practices and played the harlot in their deeds. Therefore, the anger of the Lord kindled against them. Then one day He gave them into the hands of other nations, to those who hated Israel. Israel was thus subdued under their power, even though many times God would try and deliver them. Psalms 106:39-42*

On the other hand, Ancient Rome never made any apology for its various perversions, including homosexuality, and fell because of its ever-increasing debauchery, overconfidence, and false views of God. Even though there was a core of Christians ministering to Rome before it fell, its overwhelming love of itself and sin, weakened it. By God's will, Rome was allowed to be defeated by lesser powers. After which it disintegrated and never recovered.

Whether our fate will be that of Israel or Rome, I do not know, but either outcome will bring great heartache to every American, including Christians. This will be sad because we started out so well as a nation by trusting God and His Scriptures for the decisions we made. The testimonies of Washington, Adams, Lincoln, Madison, Rush, Webster, and so many other American leaders of the past are proof of this. Let our individual testimonies end up being like these leaders, not like those who have seized control of America today.

This chapter is based on 18 verses in 9 passages of Scripture

Footnotes

1. Thomas George [editor], *God governs the Affairs of Men, Benjamin Franklin*, (The Greatest Message of All-time, Great-messages.com).
2. William J. Johnson, *George Washington the Christian* (New York, Forgotten Books/ Abingdon Press, 1919), pages 28-31.
3. Natalie Nichols, *Is America a Christian Nation? More Quotes from Our Founders: John Adams,* (Internet, Americana, May 10, 2010) *Note- Two quotes are combined into one.
4. Franklin Graham, Quote *by Abraham Lincoln* (Washington D.C., Inaugural Invocation of President George W. Bush, January 20th, 2001)
5. L.H. Butterfield, editor, *Letters of Benjamin Rush*, (Princeton: The American Philosophical Society, 1951), Volume I page 414.
6. Why-the-bible.com, *Daniel Webster*, (Internet, The Bible-Quotes from Famous Men).
7. Christian Quotes, *James Madison Christian Quote about Learning,* (Published in Christian Education Quotes, February 12th, 2012).
8. Erasing 76 Crimes, *St. Paul's Foundation for International Reconciliation*, (Published on the internet, 2012).

Chapter 12

Hollywood and the Media's Push

What should Christians do about Hollywood and the media's push for the acceptance of the LGBT agenda?

> *Woe to those who call evil good and good evil… for the wrath of God is revealed from heaven against all ungodliness and unrighteousness,… particularly for men who suppress the truth in unrighteousness Romans 1:18 & Isaiah 5:20 (RBK)*

Note: As stated in the introduction, when using the term Hollywood, I am not referring to the city, or even the people that live in this Southern California town, but to those who make up the entertainment industry. In particular, it is those who oppose what the Bible teaches about homosexuality, transgender people, and many other styles of reproachable living. Hollywood, in general, stands for worldly and non-Biblical values.

The 16th chapter of the book of Revelation describes where Armageddon will take place in the Jezreel Valley in Israel. It is the last battle fought in the world before Christ returns. This valley is historically famous because so many past battles between nations and powers were fought there. The reason for this is the valley sat in the middle of the main trade routes that linked two of the most populated and significant areas of the ancient world. Whoever ruled this valley had a strong influence on the people of that day, especially in advocating what was believed. Solomon, one of Israel's greatest kings, ruled this valley for an era, which made Israel not only very wealthy but also influential as it controlled the flow of ideologies.

In a parallel way, the entertainment industry (Hollywood) and the media of today are like those who controlled the Jezreel Valley in ancient days. What they advocate through their films, TV productions, talk shows, internet, music, and newscasts (real or fake), has made them wealthy. It has also made them renown and amazingly effective in influencing world values.

To stand against Hollywood and the media and what they promote can be very challenging and even humiliating. These powerful industries are filled with many who are popular, physically attractive, talented, and well-spoken. Their incredible communication skills alone can easily defeat an opponent. They also have significant control of many venues to which most of us are drawn, like radio, the movies, TV broadcasts, music, and the internet. Consequently, Christians who stand up for God's Word against Hollywood and the media on issues like homosexuality or transgender change can easily become outdebated and overwhelmed, if not adequately prepared.

However, with a good deal of faith, courage, knowledge of God's Word, and an understanding of the strategies Hollywood and the media employ, there is hope. Not only to survive Hollywood's assaults but to win all of the battles God has for us to win. After all, did the Lord not say we will overcome the world?

> *You are from God... and have overcome them; because greater is the Lord who is in you than he who is in the world. I John 4:4*

The entertainment industry is not only smart and motivated but absorbed with the pursuit of fame, recognition, and glory. This produces a community that becomes self-centered, prideful, and egotistical over time. Only a few of the famous and acknowledged have escaped this outcome. And to you, I say, "Way to go!"

Arguably, the Academy Awards symbolize Hollywood's grandest achievements and provide a view into its true character. Those who attend the Academy Awards night typically dress up and project themselves as the most beautiful, intelligent, wonderful, and desirable people in the world. Why? They want to be in the spotlight, to be admired, adored, respected, talked about, and even worshiped, if possible.

At the end of the awards evening, individual pursuits for fame and glory expire. Some win Oscars, but most don't. The winners are remembered for a few weeks but soon forgotten by most who watched them that evening. Test yourself on this: do you remember who won the best actor or actress award two years ago or how about just this last year? Who were the runners-up? Do you recollect any of them? The point is that what Hollywood does is short-lived, forgotten, and fleeting because its pursuits are mostly focused only on its own recognition, glory, and wealth. The Bible strongly speaks against such pursuits, because they will destroy the soul (*Ezekiel 16:15-17; Matthew 6:19-21, 24; Matthew 7:13-14*). Yet many people let Hollywood and its celebrities and representatives tell us what is true and what to believe. What a tragedy: the least qualified teach us, through worldly glitter, what is good/best in life!

I still watch the Academy Awards each year, but I view it differently now to lessen the objectionable or irrelevant portions. I record it first and then watch it after about an hour into the program. That way I can fast forward through the emcee's off-color jokes and comments, the political rants of the winners, the boring acceptance speeches, and, of course, the commercials.

The segment of the program I do like is the Memoriam Tribute. This part of the program is dedicated to those in Hollywood who have passed away during the last year. It is usually very dramatic and emotional, but also short. As important as some of these celebrities were to Hollywood only a few seconds is slotted for each of them. A portrait or short film clip of what they did is about all they get. Of course, there are exceptions for those who were more popular.

The point is that these celebrities are remembered for only a few seconds, or a minute at best, and then they fade away quickly from most of our memories like those who had just won Oscars that evening. What these deceased Hollywood stars advocated or led others to believe during their lifetimes is over, just like the earthly applause and adoration they once pursued. Upon their deaths, they have only one person to impress and gain applause from, and that is God, their creator. And as God said numerous times throughout His written Word, they, like everyone in this world, will be judged according to their faith or lack of it. If they believed in Christ, as God's only provision for salvation, and repented of their sins, they will be saved. *(John 14:6)* If they did not, then their accomplishments and self-righteous pronouncements will add to the devastating pain in their judgment.

Most of the Hollywood faithful hold to the belief that homosexuality is normal and completely acceptable. In fact, those who opt for homosexuality or gender change are to be embraced, reassured, and cheered for making such a bold and "honest" choice. Needless to say, Hollywood's view is quite contrary to God's Word as shown throughout the Scriptures. *(See Chapter 1)*

God's Word and His strategies are pretty simple and straightforward and directly communicate what is true about homosexuality as well as other sins. He asks those who believe in Him to follow His directives on these issues as outlined in Scripture and then share these truths with as many as possible. If there is resistance, then we are to apply timely rebukes, reproofs, and exhortations. These should be done according to the Scriptures and the direction of the Holy Spirit, which is given to all believers. All of this is to be done in as a kind, gentle, and loving way as possible. No anger, no antagonism, no mockery, and no degrading sarcasm, just sharing the truth about homosexuality and gender change as Jesus would if He were in our place.

> *Preach the word; be ready in season and out of season; reprove, rebuke, exhort, with great patience and instruction. For the time will come when they will not endure sound doctrine; but wanting to have their ears tickled, they will accumulate for themselves teachers in accordance to their own desires. II Timothy 4:2-3*

> *God's bond-servant must not be quarrelsome, but be kind to all, able to teach, patient when wronged, with gentleness correcting those who are in opposition. II Timothy 2:22-24*

> *But the goal of our instruction is love from a pure heart...I Timothy 1:5*

In contrast, Hollywood's strategies are more subtle or sly and often based on manipulation, exploitation, and deception. Hollywood's first strategy, for instance, is to use their appeal, status, and popularity to win us over to their way of thinking. We should never forget they are not the heroic and loving figures they seem to portray on screen or in their music. In fact, in many cases, they are quite the opposite, having proven this through their multiple marriages, divorces, and affairs. Add to this, their various sexual perversions, drug and alcohol abuses, aborted babies, and suicides, and we have quite a list of questionable character flaws to consider when listening to them.

I know they are not "heroes" by personal experience because my brother was in the entertainment business for many years. During that time, I met and talked with several celebrities, sometimes just for a few minutes and at other times for longer talks over dinner. I was never tempted to follow much of what most of them believed or promoted because, morally, they were simply not very upright. They were intelligent, good-looking, charismatic, and talented, but lacked principle when it came to truthfulness, honor, and integrity. The upshot is that a majority of celebrities, music stars, and even media personalities have proven to be poor examples. Yet, they want us to trust in what they say about homosexuality and gender change. Really! Haven't they shown they can't be listened to or trusted by the lives they have lived?

The second strategy of Hollywood is to deaden our senses toward wrongdoing and make things look okay when they are not. Even though the Bible condemns practices like homosexuality, this means nothing to the Hollywood entertainment industry. Without qualms, they saturate many of their films and productions with at least one or more scenes where homosexuality or gender change is presented as normal and acceptable. Their hope is to normalize these lifestyles which make Christians look intolerant, harsh, and unloving.

They've also done this with other issues as well. Look at how they've deadened our hearts toward premarital sex, adultery, multiple sex partners, euthanasia, suicide, and recreational drug use. In the past, they were a little more cautious in promoting immoral practices like these. No more, however, for anything goes now in Hollywood. The only time Hollywood backs off to any degree is if they start losing money because of what they are advocating.

The third strategy of Hollywood is to produce stories from the Bible that are somewhat truth-based, which seems admirable but twist the truth in these narratives. They do this for audience appeal, time parameters, or in some cases where a story is too overly spiritual to present. In their revisions, they substitute exaggerated characters, fictional dialogues, and dramatic scenes untrue to the Biblical account.

When films, TV documentaries, or other similar productions claim to be based on a true story, a great deal of caution needs to be taken before believing what is presented. When I was young, I could hardly wait to see any Hollywood production that involved Biblical characters like Moses, David, and Christ. However, things have changed so much today that I am reluctant to see these types of movies. The only ones I consider watching now are those where I know the producer or director has presented an accurate portrayal of a Biblical account. The internet helps me discern this, but often it comes from the confirmation of others I know are reliable. The bottom line is that what Hollywood has done with many of its truth-based films on the Bible, is also what it does with the LGBT agenda. It takes a basic truth about God's love and says it's solely comprised of grace and acceptance. Hollywood then distorts this and concludes that God could therefore never condemn any person or group because of their sexual orientation, nor condemn any other belief or behavior. Many of Hollywood's Biblically-based films, therefore, leave out significant parts of God's love and twist it to say what they want it to say. His loving discipline and justice, for instance, are often deleted, yet according to the Scripture, these go hand-in-hand with His love, grace, and acceptance.

> ...*Have you forgotten the exhortation which is addressed to you as sons, My son, do not regard lightly the discipline of the Lord, nor faint when you are reproved by Him; For those whom the Lord loves He disciplines...It is for discipline that you endure; God deals with you as with sons; for what son is there whom his father does not discipline? But if you are without discipline, of which all have become partakers, then you are illegitimate children and not sons. Hebrews 12:5-8*

Hollywood's final strategy is to convince us that they practice unconditional love toward the LGBT community. Its version of love, however, is not the unconditional love that the Scriptures teach. Hollywood's unconditional love says, "I accept you the way you are, and I will not try and change you no matter what. You can do anything, say anything, or be any kind of person you want to be, for I will never reprimand or judge you." For the LGBT community, this is good news because they have not always been accepted by society. But this brand of unconditional love is nothing more than an enabling kind of love that does not consider the damage that can be done to oneself and others when sins are allowed to run rampant.

Hollywood's "unconditional love" is like a young girl who struggles with drug addiction until she finally dies of an overdose. Her well-intentioned mother says nothing to criticize what she is doing because she doesn't want her daughter to feel unloved. The mother pays her daughter's bills, provides a place for her to live, and accepts her as she is, hoping that this version of unconditional love will somehow triumph. It rarely does! It is not the kind of unconditional love God gives as described in the Bible.

His love goes far beyond this mother's, or Hollywood's, as it is not only filled with grace and acceptance but loving discipline, too. In essence, God's unconditional love means there is nothing He won't do for any of us, even correcting something we are doing that will destroy ourselves, like homosexuality and other sexual sins can. On top of that, God' love provides a way (forgiveness and redemption) to help us find freedom from sins like these, along with other sin plaguing us. This is something the enabling mother in this illustration, or Hollywood itself, can and never will provide.

Here is a concluding illustration of God's love. Wouldn't you grab a child, a loved one, or a friend, if they were running toward the edge of a cliff that would claim their life if they fell over? Of course you would! Sad to say though, many of us let those we know and love rush over immoral or spiritual cliffs that God has warned against in the Scriptures: cliffs of homosexuality and other LGBT practices.

Most of this chapter has focused on how to deal with Hollywood's push for acceptance of homosexuality, gender change, and the LGBT agenda. But what is the media's (the press, reporters, TV commentators, radio hosts, and journalists) take on these issues?

Much of the media walks arm and arm with Hollywood on the LGBT agenda, believing it is right and natural to be and live this way. Only a few of the more conservative members of the media disagree with this view.

When most of the media attack Christians because of our take on homosexuality, they do it in a way (using their questioning and interview skills) to discredit us. Likely, whatever we say will be taken out of context, criticized, or belittled. And should Christians keep silent when interviewed then they are tagged as scared, weak, and intolerant. Hence, either way, whether we speak openly and truthfully, or keep silent and quietly pray, we come out on the bottom with the media and those who listen to them.

If there is any solace in this, we should at least rest with the fact that the media does this with just about everyone it interviews or reports on, even the most respected and honored of our leaders. While watching a program the other night where the President was being interviewed on national TV, I could tell he was trying to be careful not to say anything that could be misquoted or taken out of context. I was not a big fan of this President, but he did a very good job talking about the person in question. Later on, as I watched other newscasts of the identical interview, I could hardly believe it was the same one, because of the way each of these stations manipulated what was said. They totally distorted the President's answer!

Sad to say, I find that even the evening news, which touts itself as being objective in its reporting tries to sway us toward their particular point of view or political persuasion. Now I look at the news differently, unless the issue is something like the weather. Instead of looking at just one station, I look at several to find a more accurate accounting and view. Therefore, be on the alert for this is the way most of the media are these days, biased, faultfinding, negative, and not always accurate, especially with Christians and their views

Last Thoughts

What can Christians do to counter the influence of Hollywood and the media? First, stop going to R-rated films, and even boycott certain films where homosexuality and other immoral behaviors are presented as normal and acceptable. Hollywood is motivated by love of fame, love of how they appear to others, but mostly love of money and wealth. If we quit supporting films that are filled with gross language, immoral acts, and anti-Christian themes, then maybe they will change what they put out on the market.

Another way to battle Hollywood influence is to support Christian films, music, and TV programs that integrate good morals into their productions. Most of these productions, if not all, refuse to promote sexually immoral behaviors like adultery, pre-marital sex, open marriages, homosexuality, and gender change because the Bible strongly condemns these practices. In their productions, sex is between a man and a woman, and always reserved for marriage. Same-sex marriages, homosexual affairs, and other like relationships and practices are not endorsed, honored, or accepted in any way shape or form.

A little more aggressive way to fight Hollywood is to alert others when we've found that homosexuality or gender change has been included in one of Hollywood's productions. Tell family members, friends, the church, and neighbors so they can avoid these shows, then encourage them to pass on the same information to others. In short, get the word out.

Use email contacts to spread the news. This can be risky, though, for not all will share our point of view or concern. However, such a step could open up new conversations with others about God and what's in the Scriptures. When sending out emails, be careful what is written, and always use the Bible to support what is communicated. In my opinion, the best and most powerful emails are those that leave readers with the Scriptures rather than just what we've said.

Remember that when we warn others through our emails, we may be contacting some who are struggling with homosexuality or gender change themselves. In respect to this, lace what is expressed with a good measure of thoughtful love, hope and resolve. And don't be surprised if some email contacts ask to be deleted because of what we've shared. Regrettably, this is sometimes the outcome when Christians stand up for God's truth on tough issues relating to homosexuality.

The last tactic to negate Hollywood's influence is to refuse to buy from companies that openly support the gay agenda. More and more companies are openly publicizing their support for gays and all those associated with them. For the most part, these companies do this because they think it helps their bottom line. In respect to this, one of my friends went online several months ago and found 379 companies that openly support same-sex marriage. As much as possible, he committed not to buy any products from these companies. His point was that even though his refusal to buy from these companies would have little impact on their profits, at least he was doing something. So, do something!

Scripture References

Ezekiel 16: 15-17 *[15]But you trusted in your beauty and played the harlot because of your fame, and you poured out your harlotries on every passer-by who might be willing. [16]You took some of your clothes, made for yourself high places of various colors and played the harlot on them, which should never come about nor happen. [17]You also took your beautiful jewels made of My gold and of My silver, which I had given you, and made for yourself male images that you might play the harlot with them.*

Matthew 6: 19-21, 24 *¹⁹Do not store up for yourselves treasures on earth, where moth and rust destroy, and where thieves break in and steal. ²⁰But store up for yourselves treasures in heaven, where neither moth nor rust destroys, and where thieves do not break in or steal; ²¹for where your treasure is, there your heart will be also. ²⁴No one can serve two masters; for either he will hate the one and love the other, or he will be devoted to one and despise the other. You cannot serve God and wealth.*

Matthew 7: 13-14 *¹³Enter through the narrow gate; for the gate is wide, and the way is broad that leads to destruction, and there are many who enter through it. ¹⁴For the gate is small and the way is narrow that leads to life, and there are few who find it.*

John 14:6 *Jesus said to him, "I am the way, and the truth, and the life; no one comes to the Father but through Me."*

This chapter is based on 21 verses in 10 passages of Scripture

Chapter 13

Reaching Out and Loving the LGBT Community

How should Christians love and reach out to the LGBT Community?

If God so loved us, we also ought to love one another. I John 4:11

    The following six attributes of God's love, when woven together and put into practice by Christians, should help those in the LGBT community find healing, peace, and lasting joy. Some of the following attributes overlap one another, but each has its separate application. There is no particular order to these attributes of His love; the first is not greater nor more important than the last.

Attribute 1: God's love is available to help all who come to Him.

Come unto Me, all who are weary and heavy-laden, and I will give you rest. Matthew 11:28

    God has invited all to come to Him for help and healing, regardless of the sin, offense, or wrongdoing. He doesn't care how many times or when we last committed a particular sin. God has said over and over in His Word that He welcomes us *AS IS*, and then goes about making us well and whole when we put our faith in Him. After His work is completed at the end of our lives, or at each stage of our lives, comes the rest we need, a rest we never thought possible.

    God wants to examine and work in us to see what He needs to do to cure us of the ills and hurts that result from sin. For some salvation is needed, which requires repentance of sin and belief in Christ. Without this, there is not a lot God will do from that point on until we make this decision. Members of the LGBT Community need to seek God's forgiveness for what they are doing and put their faith in Christ if they want to find the lasting peace only God can give.

    God is available and willing to help anyone seeking Him. Collectively as a church, we should also be available and open to others who enter our places of worship, especially those of the LGBT persuasion. Hopefully, as they come to our churches, they will find love, acceptance, friendship, the truth about God, and the truth about what they are doing from His perspective. Should they respond to Him with faith and repentance, then they will need from us all of the forgiveness, discipleship, and inclusion we can give.

Attribute 2: God's love sacrifices and endures any hurt for the sake of others.

> *Fix your eyes on Jesus, the author and perfecter of faith, who for the joy set before Him endured the cross, despised the shame and has sat down at the right hand of the throne of God. For consider Him who has endured such hostility by sinners against Himself, so that you will not grow weary and lose heart. Hebrews 12:2-3*

God has done everything to save His human creation, even those consumed with many sins and gross offenses. Christ's sacrifice on the cross to atone for these sins, no matter what they are, is evidence of this. God made such a sacrifice because He loved mankind so much that He wanted everyone to spend eternity with Him. Not even Hollywood's so-called unconditional love, which is just permissiveness, can compare to this kind of love.

Christians should, therefore, continue to minister to those in the LGBT community even if it causes them great personal sacrifice or humiliation to do so. The verbal and physical abuse Jesus endured was not enough to stop Him, nor should it stop us who have His presence and the power of the Spirit. Like Christ, we are to love the LGBT community no matter what is done to us in return, either from them directly or from those who support their lifestyle.

Attribute 3: God's love grants complete and irreversible forgiveness to those who seek it.

> *When we were dead in our sins, God made us alive with Christ. He forgave us all our sins, nailing them all to the cross. Colossians 2:13 [RBK]*

God's forgiveness is complete and irreversible and includes sins committed in the past, present, and future. After we are forgiven, God gives us a full measure of His Spirit, to guide, protect, and help us fight off sin the rest of our lives. Amazingly, the Spirit promises never to leave us no matter how many times we repeat a sin or fail. *(I John 1:9; I Corinthians 6:19; Hebrews 13:5)*

How should Christians apply this measure of forgiveness to members of the LGBT Community seeking help? The first thing is to stay in a relationship with them until they choose to accept the Lord's forgiveness. All we may be able to do during this time is to be their friend and share with them about God's forgiveness as it is laid out in Scriptures. Once they've responded, then give them the same 100% forgiveness that God gives you.

Too often Christians don't forgive others as they should, thinking that another's sin is worse than theirs. The sins of homosexual and transgender people may seem more detestable or different, but their sins are no less forgivable than any other sins. After they've believed, treat them with respect, as co-equals in the kingdom of God. Should they relapse into old ways, then come alongside and give them the help and encouragement they need, the same kind you would want if you fell back into one of your old sins.

Maybe, just maybe, the kind of forgiveness we model will be a great draw to others we are trying to reach for the kingdom. There is nothing like a good example to impact and influence others.

> *...forgive each other....just as the Lord forgave you... Colossians 3:13*

Attribute 4: God's love embraces both grace and discipline.

> *For by grace you have been saved through faith; and that not of yourselves, it is the gift of God...but if you are without discipline, of which all have become partakers, then you are illegitimate children and not sons. Ephesians 2:8 & Hebrews 12:8*

God's love combines both grace and discipline, like two sides of the same coin. The grace side of God's love is forgiveness and mercy. Upon belief and repentance, His grace is ours and can never be lost or removed. We may fail at times with God, maybe many times, or even most of the time, but He will never remove His grace from our lives. *(John 10:28)*

Additionally, His grace erases all judgments that would have come to us had our faith not been put into play. The short of this is that when we die, and we will, we will skip the judgment others will have to go through because they did not take God's offer of salvation. *(John 3:16-18)*

The other side of the coin is God's discipline, which comprises a variety of caring and corrective measures to help us abandon and stay clear of sinful ways. Ways that will stunt our spiritual growth as Christians or worse yet, keep us out of God's kingdom if accompanied by disbelief in Him and an unrepentant heart.

God's discipline for homosexual and transgender people who refuse to believe Him and repent is to do very little. Instead, God lets them reap the consequences of their own actions by allowing each to experience different measures of guilt, shame, unhappiness, hopelessness, regret, lack of fulfillment, loss of self-esteem, damaged ties with family and friends, sickness, and even death. The hope is that in their misery and dissatisfaction, they will turn to Him. If they do, then they will receive a limitless measure of His grace. And from that grace can come incredible joy, peace, and satisfaction. If they don't respond but continue in their homosexuality or gender change, then the negative effects listed above will only worsen over time.

Christians, who revert to old sinful habits like homosexuality and gender change, continue in His grace and do not lose their salvation or His presence. However, these wayward believers will be called into account by God through their conscience, consequences, and what other Christians urge them to do.

According to the guidelines of Scripture, Christians are called upon to help one another abandon new and reoccurring sins. They do this by praying, being a good example themselves, and re-teaching what is true and not true from God's Word. If this works and a wayward believer recuperates from a sin, then there is nothing further to be done. If it doesn't work, then more exacting rebukes, reproofs, and reprimands are in order from fellow believers.

Should all of these measures fail, then these fallen believers may need to be separated from the church for a while until repentance is realized. The goal of the separation is not to hurt them, but to get them back to trusting God for this part of their lives. For this sin, like every other sin, can ruin a Christian walk if not addressed with remorse and forgiveness. *(II Timothy 4:2; Hebrews 12:5-8; Matthew 18:15-18; I Timothy 5:20; Galatian 5:1; I Corinthians 5:9-11,13; II Thessalonians 3:6, 14,15; Proverbs 9:7-8)*

Once their restoration has been accomplished, then the whole church is to rejoice and begin to treat these repaired and reinstated believers as if they had never sinned. To not forgive them, after God has, is a sin that we should avoid. The Lord's Prayer and many other portions of Scripture say, "Forgive us our trespasses, as we forgive others

The whole point of this attribute is to apply both grace and discipline according to each situation, not one over the other. Only the Scriptures and other more mature and seasoned believers can help you with this.

Attribute 5: God doesn't force His love but does everything possible to help us understand and receive it.

God's love gives everyone the freedom to accept or reject His love. He forces no one to love Him in return, accept His plan of salvation, believe His Scriptures, or receive His forgiveness of sin. To help sway us toward His love, God has shown each of us what He is like within our hearts, as well as what He inspired to be written in the Scriptures. From the beginning, God reveals to everyone a sense of His presence through our conscience, feelings, and intelligence. If there are any exceptions beyond this, God's grace or judgment will abound. *(Romans 2:14-16)*

To the day that we die, God will continue to do everything possible to reach and save each of us, but He won't take away our free will in the process. God does this because He has an incredible love for mankind. If we refuse His love to the end of our lives, then His love ends for us at that point and judgment begins.

The Lord is not slow about His promise, as some count slowness, but is patient toward you, not wishing for any to perish but for all to come to repentance. II Peter 3:9

He who believes in Him is not judged; he who does not believe has been judged already because he has not believed in the name of only begotten Son of God. John 3:18

We might say, "Well, that doesn't sound like unconditional love at all!" In a way, God's love isn't unconditional because He will not just take anyone into heaven unless they've demonstrated faith and repentance. If God did permit the unrepentant and unfaithful, then heaven would be no more than another version of this world, distorted by sin, selfishness, and unbelief. Therefore, God's unconditional love is tied up in doing everything possible to get us free from sin and into His kingdom and heaven.

As Christians, how do we apply God's love for the LGBT Community? We start by asking ourselves if we are doing everything possible to bring them into the kingdom of God. Yet, while trying, whether it is through prayer, the building of a stronger relationship, presenting the Gospel at opportune times, and even sharing the truth about what they are doing to themselves and others, we must realize we can't force God's love on them. It is always for them to decide. Sometimes, they choose wisely and sometimes not.

So, be as diligent as you can in your ministry with the gay and transgender person, but at the same time, relax, for it is up to them to respond to the Lord.

Attribute 6: God's love sometimes chooses one love over another

> *When the Son of Man comes, and all the angels with him, he will sit on his glorious throne. All the nations will be gathered before him, and he will separate the people as a shepherd separates the sheep from the goats. He will put the sheep on his right and the goats on his left. Then He said to those on his right, 'Come, you who are blessed by my Father; take your inheritance, for the kingdom, is prepared for you.' Then he will say to those on his left, 'Depart from me, you who are cursed." Matthew 25:31-34, 41 (RBK)*

Just as God decides who will go to heaven and who won't, similarly Christians may have to choose one love over another. If we have tried without success to win over those in the LGBT Community, then it may be time to move onto others who also need God. By doing this, we end up choosing a latter love over a former one. Jesus' parable of the sower supports a move like this, for He told His disciples when throwing out the seeds of the Gospel to look for those who respond, whom He called good ground. *(Matthew 13:18-23)* In another instance, Jesus told his disciples in Matthew 10 to go into a village with the Gospel, and if the people responded then stay. If they didn't respond, then the disciples were to move on.

In another application of choosing one love over another, there may be gays we have come to know and love that might influence or threaten the well-being of others we love. We don't abandon our gay friends or family members because we dislike them, but for the sake of the others we love who are at risk. For instance, our children may have schoolmates or neighbor friends who are gay or have changed their gender. In the midst of this, we should be trying to teach our children how to reach those schoolmates and neighbor friends for the Gospel. But by doing this, we put our kids at risk, exposing them to some pretty carnal, sinful, and questionable behaviors. So, what do we do?

Let me share what I did with my children's neighborhood friends who were definitely not Christians and a bit worldly-minded. First of all, I taught my kids how to share a very simple Gospel and how to love their neighborhood friends by just being their friend. However, my wife and I did not let our children be alone with them at any time. If they wanted to play together as kids love to do, then it had to be done at our home, or where Myrna and I were in the vicinity. That way, we were able to monitor and correct anything that was being said or done.

The point to all of this is that sometimes our love for gay or transgender friends, co-workers, neighbors, or relatives, may have to take a back seat to others we love who are either more responsive to God's truth, or in need of protection from those living an LGBT style of life.

Last Thoughts

If I were to weave these six attributes of God's love together to reach gay and transgender people, here is how it would look for me. I would try and be available to them in any way possible, be their friend, and be willing to suffer humiliation should it result. Then I would focus on Christ's message of salvation and grace, but also talk with them about their sexual sins. If they were unbelievers and did accept Christ and His forgiveness, then I would make every effort to be just as forgiving and forgetful of their sins, as He is. If they are Christians that fell back into homosexuality or gender change, or any derivatives of these sins, then I would apply more of the discipline mentioned in the Scriptures to get them to stop their relapse. In the midst of all of this, I would never try and force God's love on them, whether Christian or not. True and lasting love never has to be forced. Finally, if my love for them had no results after a long time of trying, or I found they were damaging others with their influence, then I would suspend my relationship with them for a while until things changed.

Scripture References

I John 1:9 *If we confess our sins, He is faithful and righteous to forgive us our sins and to cleanse us from all unrighteousness.*

I Corinthians 6:19 *Do you not know that your body is a temple of the Holy Spirit who is in you, whom you have from God, and that you are not your own?*

Hebrews 13:5 *... He Himself has said, "I will never desert you, nor will I ever forsake you."*

John 10:28 *I give eternal life to them, and they will never perish, and no one will snatch them out of My hand.*

John 3:16-18 *[16]For God so loved the world, that He gave His only begotten Son, that whoever believes in Him shall not perish, but have eternal life, [17]for God did not send the Son into the world to judge the world, but that the world might be saved through Him. [18]He who believes in Him is not judged; he who does not believe has been judged already because he has not believed in the name of the only begotten Son of God.*

II Timothy 4:2 *Preach the word; be ready in season and out of season; reprove, rebuke, exhort, with great patience and instruction.*

Hebrews 12:5-8 *[5]My son, do not regard lightly the discipline of the Lord, nor faint when you are reproved by Him; [6]For those whom the Lord loves He disciplines, and He scourges every son whom He receives. [7]It is for* discipline that you endure; God deals with you as with sons; for what son is there whom his father does not discipline? ^{8}But if you are without discipline, of which all have become partakers, then you are illegitimate children and not sons.

Matthew 18 15-18 ^{15}If your brother sins, go and show him his fault in private; if he listens to you, you have won your brother. ^{16}But if he does not listen to you, take one or two more with you, so that by the mouth of two or three witnesses every fact may be confirmed. ^{17}If he refuses to listen to them, tell it to the church; and if he refuses to listen even to the church, let him be to you as a Gentile and a tax collector.

I Timothy 5:20 Those who continue in sin, rebuke in the presence of all, so that the rest also will be fearful of sinning.

Galatians 6:1 Brethren, even if anyone is caught in any trespass, you who are spiritual, restore such a one in a spirit of gentleness; each one looking to yourself so that you too will not be tempted.

I Corinthians 5:9-11,13 ^{9}I wrote you in my letter not to associate with immoral people; ^{10}I did not at all mean with the immoral people of this world...for then you would have to go out of the world. ^{11}But actually, I wrote to you not to associate with any so-called brother if he is an immoral person...not even to eat with such a one. ^{13}...Remove the wicked man from among yourselves.

II Thessalonians 3:6,14,15 ^{6}Now we command you, brethren, in the name of our Lord Jesus Christ, that you keep away from every brother who leads an unruly life and not according to the tradition which you received from us. ^{14}If anyone does not obey our instruction in this letter, take special note of that person and do not associate with him, so that he will be put to shame. ^{15}Yet do not regard him as an enemy but admonish him as a brother.

Proverbs 9:7-8 ^{7}If you correct a scoffer he will dishonor and hate you, and if you reprove a wicked man, he will throw insults at you. ^{8}Thus, do not reprove a scoffer but reprove rather a wise man for he will love you. (RBK)

Romans 2: 14-16 [14]*For when Gentiles who do not have the Law do instinctively the things of the Law, these, not having the Law, are a law to themselves,* [15]*in that they show the work of the Law written in their hearts, their conscience bearing witness and their thoughts alternately accusing or else defending them,* [16]*on the day when, according to my gospel, God will judge the secrets of men through Christ Jesus.*

Matthew 13:18-23 [18]*Hear then the parable of the sower.* [19]*When anyone hears the word of the kingdom and does not understand it, the evil one comes and snatches away what has been sown in his heart. This is the one on whom seed was sown beside the road.* [20]*The one on whom seed was sown on the rocky places, this is the man who hears the word and immediately receives it with joy;* [21]*yet he has no firm root in himself but is only temporary, and when affliction or persecution arises because of the word, immediately he falls away.* [22]*And the one on whom seed was sown among the thorns, this is the man who hears the word, and the worry of the world and the deceitfulness of wealth choke the word, and it becomes unfruitful.* [23]*And the one on whom seed was sown on the good soil, this is the man who hears the word and understands it; who indeed bears fruit and brings forth, some a hundredfold, some sixty, and some thirty.*

This chapter is based on 50 verses in 25 passages of Scripture

Conclusion

Approaching Tough Dilemmas

If any of you lacks wisdom, you should ask God, who gives generously to all without finding fault, and it will be given to you (James 1:5)

The conclusion ends by applying the principles within this book to the following questions and real-life dilemmas.

Should I attend a wedding where two gays or transgender people are getting married?

First of all, I would determine if the gays or transgender people are Christian or non-Christian. If a Christian couple, I would not attend because it supports a sin that is strongly condemned in the Bible and one of which they should be aware. To go, would validate them in their sinful choice.

If the marrying gay couple were non-Christian friends or non-believing relatives, then before I accepted their invitation, I would clarify to them what I Scripturally believed regarding their homosexuality or transgender state. If that were okay with them, then I would go to their wedding out of love. By loving them in this way, yet not accepting their sin, I could open up new doors down the road to talk with them about God and His teachings.

Should I hire a gay or transgender person?

If I owned a business, I would not hesitate to hire gays or those who have changed their gender, as long as they knew what I believed and why I believed it. Once again, this is an application of loving sinners, yet standing against their sinful lifestyles. I would treat them with as much love as possible as their employer, hoping that one day by doing this they would consider God and invite Christ into their lives.

Should I hire a gay or transgender person to work in a Christian school, Christian organization, or at Church?

I would not hire homosexuals or those who have changed their transgender, or anyone else committed to these kinds of sinful lifestyles to be part of my staff in a Christian ministry. The employees in all Christian ministries are to be examples of the Biblical truths taught to others. By a homosexual or transgender person's admission, neither follows God's truth in this area of their lives.

While the church should always be as diverse as possible and include people of all races, walks of life, professions, and economic status, it is not a free-for-all where the staff lives and believes how they want. The church, the true church that is, should expect all employees, and its leaders, in particular, to not only teach God's truth to others but to live by those truths as well.

Should I invite a gay couple in my neighborhood over for dinner?

Yes, how else are you going to minister and get to know them?

Should I allow a gay couple to sleep in the same room at my home?

For both Christians and non-Christians, I would not allow them to sleep overnight in the same room at my home. For the Christian, this would be a rebuke of their sin. For the non-Christian, it would be a moral statement and stance to them that what they are doing is wrong according to the Scriptures I follow.

How should a youth director handle a retreat where gay or young people who have changed their gender, want to come? How could the facilities be arranged if they attend?

This is the most difficult question to answer because it involves parents, children, young people, church reputation, and Biblical truth.

Here are some of my thoughts:

If the retreat is with young children of elementary school or junior high age, I would not allow a gay or child who has changed their gender, to come. I wouldn't because the Christian children under my care would not be mature enough to handle such a complicated and spiritual issue. In response, there might be parents who cry discrimination, but I would stick with my decision. As much as I would like to reach a gay or transgender child for the kingdom through a retreat, I wouldn't, for the sake of other children's welfare, faith, and future understanding of God's Word.

If the young people under my supervision were in high school or older, I would consider letting a gay or transgender student come as long as the entire group knew the circumstances. The group would have to know what Scripture teaches and why, how to love a gay or transgender student, and how to lead him or her to Christ.

The general purpose of most Christian retreats is to help Christian young people grow and develop in their faith. In having a gay or transgender student at a retreat would certainly provide the opportunity for that to happen.

In this retreat situation, where they are welcomed, I would give the gay or transgender student their own time in the bathroom so the privacy of other kids would be honored and protected. The gay student would sleep in the cabin with the rest of his or her gender as long as a counselor was on site. The transgender student would need to bunk in the cabin of the gender with which they were born. There might be pushback from the parents on both sides on this, and if it could not be resolved without hurt or confusion, then I would cancel or postpone the retreat for another time.

Last Thought

Sad to say, it is we who make a mistake and bring confusion, conflict, and misunderstanding to our world when we mess around with God's morality as taught and defined in the Scripture, especially when we try to change or alter His predetermined sexual design intended for each one of us.

Appendix
(Questions from the Chapters)

Chapter 1

What does Scripture teach Christians about homosexuality and transgender people?

Chapter 2

Can a person be born or destined to be homosexual?

What place does our sin nature play when it comes to homosexuality or changing gender?

Is homosexuality or gender change a gray area in the Bible, or on the proverbial bubble?

With the truth in view about being born with a sin nature, rather than being born homosexual or of the wrong gender, how should we treat those who believe this about themselves?

Chapter 3

Did God ever indicate in the Scriptures that homosexuality or changing gender was bad in a previous era, but transitioned to be okay today?

Since God brings guilt to all who sin, why is it that some gays seemingly feel freer or less guilty about themselves when they "come out"?

How should we relate or minister to someone who has "come out" about their homosexuality or gender change?

In addition to wanting to feel free about their homosexuality, do gays or those who change their gender have other reasons for "coming out"?

If we as Christians feel uncomfortable with someone who is gay or has changed their gender, what should we do?

Chapter 4

What is meant when Christians are called homophobic or tagged as discriminatory toward gays and transgender people?

Is standing against gays or those who have changed their gender the same as standing against someone of a different race or color?

How would our early America leaders have resolved the issues of homosexuality and changing gender? What would have been their guiding references?

Chapter 5

Is one set of sins greater than another when it comes to salvation?

Is the practice of homosexuality or gender change worse than other sins in the Bible?

What grouping of sins is homosexuality associated within the Scriptures?

Why are homosexuality and changing gender sinful and rejected by God when these sexually-oriented behaviors seemingly don't harm anyone as other sins do?

Chapter 6

What did Jesus teach about homosexuality?

What was God's original physical and psychological make-up of a man and a woman?

What should we do if we are told to follow a particular law about homosexuality that runs counter to our faith?

What did Paul the Apostle think about homosexuality; how did he describe it?

How would Jesus have responded to gays, the effeminate, cross-dressers, and even the transgender of this current generation?

Chapter 7

Is it a coincidence that disease and illness sometimes follow immoral and sexual misconduct?

Does it happen that innocent victims sometimes suffer a sexual disease because of the unfaithfulness or actions of others?

Chapter 8

How is it possible that some Christians claim that homosexuality and changing gender are okay, and other Christians don't?

What is the best definition of a genuine Christian according to the Scriptures?

What are some worldly opinions about who qualifies as a Christian?

How does God convict us when we sin?

How should Christians work with Christians and non-Christians who identify themselves as homosexual?

Chapter 9

Is it right to judge members of the LGBT Community for their practices?

What set of circumstances determine if Christians are to judge others?

How do we determine if a sin is a sin?

Why did the Apostle Paul encourage Christians to make others accountable for their sins, yet criticized some for judging?

When making others accountable for their sins, should we have a different approach with those who are Christians versus non-Christians?

Is it better to be gentle than confrontational when approaching others about their sins?

Chapter 10

How do churches who support homosexuality and transgender change feel about Christians who don't?

Does the Scripture stand behind churches that make homosexuality and transgender change an acceptable lifestyle?

What part of God's grace do liberally-minded churches usually delete in their message to the LGBT community?

Can a Christian de-convert from his or her original beliefs?

What can we learn from the churches of the '60s to help reach the LGBT community of today?

Chapter 11

With the current spiritual state of most American leaders, what's next in the decisions they will make for us as a country?

Why has God allowed homosexuality and changing gender to prevail in the current judicial rulings?

What can we do today to constitutionally remove Federal judges and Supreme Court Justices that run counter to what a majority of Americans want for their laws?

What do many other nations throughout the world feel about homosexuality, same-sex marriage, and changing gender?

Chapter 12

How can Christians counter the influence of Hollywood and the media; what can they expect if they stand up against them?

Knowing what we do about Hollywood, why do we let those in this entertainment industry tell us what is true about this life?

What do a majority of Hollywood's celebrities, representatives, and spokesmen advocate about homosexuality and gender change, and what are their strategies to convince us of what to believe?

Why does Hollywood slip scenes of homosexuality or gender change into its productions, particularly films that have nothing to do with these practices or lifestyles?

How does Hollywood's version of unconditional love differ from the Scriptures?

What are the underlying purposes and tactics of the media when attacking Christians for their views?

Chapter 13

What is God's version of accepting us *AS IS*?

What must homosexuals and those who change their gender do to be healed and accepted by God?

As a church, should we be available and open to those of the LGBT persuasion?

If gays and any of their offshoots were to respond to Christ's message at our church, what will they need from us?

What level of abuse should Christians endure from those who humiliate them for their views on the LGBT community?

How does the grace and discipline sides of God's love work, are both necessary when working with those in the LGBT community?

Is it possible God's love may not be the same unconditional love the world advocates?

What can you do to reach out to children who are gay or who have changed their gender, while at the same time protecting your children from their influence?

Conclusion

Should I attend a wedding where two gays or two who have changed their gender are getting married?

Should I hire a gay or a transgender person?

Should I invite a gay couple in my neighborhood over for dinner?

Should I allow a gay couple to sleep overnight in the same room at my home?

How should a youth director handle a retreat where a young person who is gay or has changed his or her gender wants to attend? How can facilities be arranged for them and the others attending?

www.ingramcontent.com/pod-product-compliance
Lightning Source LLC
Chambersburg PA
CBHW021957290426
44108CB00012B/1112